A GUIDEBOOK TO THE SAN GABRIEL MOUNTAINS
OF CALIFORNIA

A GUIDEBOOK TO THE SAN GABRIEL MOUNTAINS OF CALIFORNIA

BY RUSS LEADABRAND

THE WARD RITCHIE PRESS · LOS ANGELES

First edition published May, 1963. Revised edition, with additional material on trails and new map published January, 1964

Third Printing, July 1964

Library of Congress Catalog Card Number 63-16988

IT TOOK MANY TO MAKE THE
BIG DREAM COME TRUE:
CHARLES FREEMAN, MURCO
RINGNALDA, BILL FEARN, FRED
RUNYON, PATRICE MANAHAN,
AND BARBARA.

Cover illustration is of the Astronomical complex atop Mt. Wilson; tall towers are solar telescopes. Used by courtesy of California Institute of Technology. Frontispiece is one of the patriarchal limber pines atop Mt. Baden-Powell. Photo by U.S. Forest Service.

COPYRIGHT © 1963 BY RUSS LEADABRAND

REVISED EDITION © 1964 BY RUSS LEADABRAND

DISTRIBUTED EXCLUSIVELY BY LANE BOOK COMPANY
MENLO PARK, CALIFORNIA

CONTENTS

PAGE

I. *Introduction* 1

II. *Introduction to the Angeles National Forest* . . . 4

III. *Angeles Crest Highway* 7

IV. *Arroyo Seco* 24

V. *Mount Wilson Road* 25

VI. *Chantry Flats Road—Big Santa Anita* 27

VII. *San Gabriel Canyon Road* 30

VIII. *Glendora Mountain Road* 38

IX. *Mt. Baldy Road* 39

X. *Lytle Creek Road* 43

XI. *Cajon to Valyermo Road* 47

XII. *Little Rock Reservoir Road* 55

XIII. *Angeles Forest Highway* 57

XIV. *Soledad Canyon Road* 62

XV. *Mint Canyon Road* 67

XVI. *Bouquet Canyon Road* 71

XVII. *San Francisquito Canyon Road* 75

XVIII. *Elizabeth Lake Canyon Road* 81

XIX. *Old Ridge Route* 84

XX. *Leona Valley, Elizabeth Lake, Pine Canyon Roads* . 89

XXI. *Little Tujunga* 92

XXII. *Big Tujunga* 94

XXIII. *Mt. Lowe* 98

XXIV. *Trails* 101

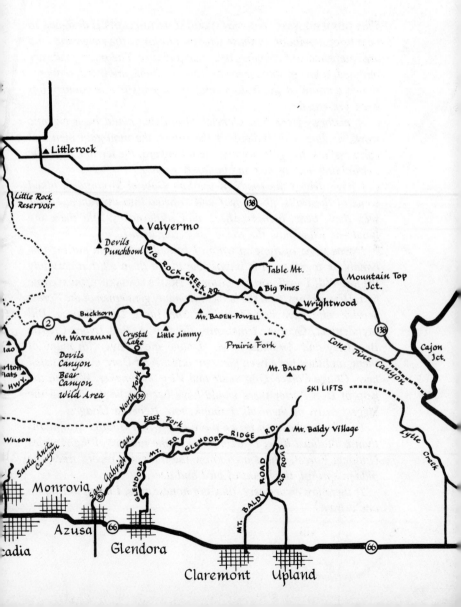

This GUIDEBOOK TO THE SAN GABRIEL MOUNTAINS *is designed to be a brief handbook to those who do not know the range and who are interested in becoming better acquainted. The main roads are outlined, a few of the dozens of trails available are listed, a microscopic amount of the history and the legends of the country has been presented.*

A history of the San Gabriel Mountains could be a gigantic work, dealing with Indians of the range, the mountain men and early settlers, the gold booms, the hiking era, the terrible fires, the pyramiding bulk of fact and fiction born here.

I have driven the roads of the San Gabriel Mountains, hiked some of the trails, flown over and crawled into the range. I have seen deer, bear, bighorn sheep and rattlesnakes. Still there are hundreds who know the range far better than I.

It was some of these to whom I turned for help in putting this handbook together. It is impossible to list them all, but certainly the late Will Thrall, former editor of TRAILS MAGAZINE, *must come first. His work inspired the book. The many gentlemen of the Forest Service who have helped include Sim Jarvi, Dick Droege, Bill Mendenhall, George Armstrong, Ed Corpe, Ben Lyon, Charlie Beardsley and Anselmo Lewis. I have spent days with many of them, and they have been pleasant days. Walt Dorn must be listed here, Chuck Colver, Odo Stade and Virg Shoemaker. Without the help of Don Porter there would have been no book; his was the biggest assist of them all. I thank, too, Rebecca Hodges.*

For those who wish to see more of the San Gabriel Mountains than is outlined here, I direct them to the rangers of the Angeles National Forest. These men know the trails, the record trees, the hidden springs, the haunt of bird and deer.

If there are errors here, they are honest ones; I mean to lead no one astray.

I INTRODUCTION

The San Gabriel Mountains of Southern California offer emphatic contrasts: desert views and tall timber, lakes, campgrounds, fishing streams and ski resorts.

THE SAN GABRIEL MOUNTAINS of Southern California are part of the great high barrier arc that separates the Mojave Desert from the fair sea-bounded coastlands. Roughly east and west the range runs, with pronounced terminations at the east with Cajon Pass and 100 miles to the west at the natural trough followed by U.S. Highway 99. An older name for the range is the Sierra Madre Mountains.

It is mountain country of emphatic contrasts. The north rim is footed mainly along the edge of the Antelope Valley, a projection of the Mojave Desert country. The high ridges reach to 10,000 feet and some shady spots frequently know patches of old snow and ice from winter to winter. There are man-made and natural lakes. There are streams—snow and spring fed—that run throughout the driest seasons. There are stands of rough-barked ruddy cedars, weather-grated limber pines, giant pines and record oaks. Recreation resources range from rock climbing, fishing, hunting, hiking, horseback riding, snow sports, to simpler things like motoring, bird watching and sightseeing.

Situated within easy driving distance of the population centers of the Southland, the San Gabriel Mountains can be reached by a network of fine mountain highways. For more adventurous explorers there are numerous unpaved Forest Service truck trails open to the public most of the year. These narrow byways frequently lead back to camping sites, picnic spots, hiking trails and view-

Blue-green pine, fir and cedar stand on these high slopes of the San Gabriel Mountains. Brown bear and bighorn sheep live in the wilder areas.

points of particular charm. These roads can be driven or hiked.

Most of the San Gabriel Mountains lie within the boundaries of the Angeles National Forest, a federal preserve that manages and protects close to 700,000 acres of mountain country, roughly one fourth of the land area of Los Angeles County.

Because of the constant threat of fire—major fires have burned in the San Gabriel Mountains in each of the twelve months during recent years—certain sections of the range are closed in summer. But with hundreds of miles of roads, riding and hiking trails available even by summer, there is still plenty of the unusual to see and enjoy.

For the San Gabriel Mountains do provide the unusual. The range sits directly atop the awesome San Andreas earthquake fault, and geologists claim that these mountains are the most fractured, most shattered in California.

Here there are strange rock formations to explore and climb —like Vasquez Rocks and Devil's Punchbowl.

There are bighorn sheep in the high country.

The mountains boast a fat file of strange tales and historic legends.

But the fine mountain roads beckon, and thousands of Southern California's residents and visitors call on the range each month. There are many picnic sites, frequent campgrounds, resorts, historic landmarks, and endless attractive views.

But the best thing about the San Gabriel Mountains is the mountains themselves: rockribbed, burned over or green with young chaparral, sharp-etched against the blue winter sky or misty and phantom in the creeping, canyon-following arms of smog. The sights and sounds, the wash of wind, the medicinal and restoring scents—these are the things that have lured the traveler into the range for hundreds of years.

May it ever be thus.

II INTRODUCTION TO THE ANGELES NATIONAL FOREST

The Angeles National Forest, created in 1892, manages 691,052 mountain acres, roughly a quarter of the land area of Los Angeles County, and looks after the watershed and recreation values there.

THE ANGELES NATIONAL FOREST—the second in the United States set aside to preserve certain wild woodland and foothill values—was born on December 20, 1892, the "San Gabriel Timberland Reserve." On March 2, 1907, the title of the preserve was changed to the San Gabriel National Forest.

In the beginning the Angeles National Forest included the mountain regions of the San Bernardino range. The San Bernardino National Forest was cut from the Angeles and became a separate entity in 1925.

There are five districts of the Angeles, the fifth and newest being created this year. These are: the Arroyo Seco, with headquarters in Pasadena; the Mt. Baldy, with headquarters in Glendora; the Valyermo, with headquarters at Valyermo; the Saugus, with headquarters at Newhall; and the new Tujunga, with headquarters at Sylmar.

Headquarters for the entire forest is located at 1015 North Lake Avenue, in Pasadena.

Visitors with questions should inquire at district ranger offices, or manned forest stations. Here they can get fire permits, permits for collection of forest products like pine cones, mistletoe, firewood, manzanita, building stone, etc., when such are available. Ranger office personnel can also answer questions on mineral

4

claims, closed areas, special use permits. Here is usually the best place to inquire about the most recent condition of truck trails or hiking and riding trails. Forest stations distribute free maps of their district.

Most rangers in the field are on patrol duty, there to answer your questions, to help you better enjoy your visit to the forest.

The problems of the managers of the Angeles National Forest are many and complex. For years the Angeles National Forest has been one of the most heavily used of all the nation's National Forests. In addition to a staggering load of motorists and hikers, fire is a frequent visitor. Most of the steep, rubbly slopes of the San Gabriel Mountains are covered with chaparral—a broad term that includes a number of kinds of scrub trees and brush, all highly inflammable, that are able to survive in the long seasons of drought. Fire fighting in such terrain, against such fuels, is costly and exhausting, and strange weapons against fire—such as the aerial bomber—have been invented and used.

Many truck trails in the Forest are permanently closed to public travel by automobiles. These roads are gated, chained, or have a locked cable across them. These closures should not be ignored. The closed road is closed for a good reason: it leads onto private or classified property; the road is dangerous and not patrolled; the road is within the seasonal fire closure. There are many other, open roads in the Forest that can be enjoyed.

During the season from May 1 to December 15 it is unlawful to smoke in the Forest except at campgrounds, resorts or designated smoking areas along the highway.

Drivers of four-wheel-drive vehicles and specially geared motor scooters who wish to tackle difficult pieces of terrain within the Forest should first apply for permission at a district ranger office. There are areas within the Forest where it is against the law to discharge firearms. Almost all streams and lakes—except private

5

lakes—are open to trout fishing the year around. Many are stocked regularly by the State Department of Fish and Game.

There are no up-to-date hiking maps of the San Gabriel Mountains country. Topographical maps issued by the U. S. Geological Survey, and the district maps issued by the Forest Service contain the most useful information on trails. But many older trails in the mountain country have become dangerous. If you plan to hike or horseback ride an old or an unfamiliar trail, best check first with a Forest ranger.

Overnight camping is allowed in the Angeles National Forest only in places designated as campgrounds. Fires are permitted in most campground and picnic areas where stoves are provided and when the user has a fire permit. Open fires are not allowed. In some heavily used campgrounds in season of greatest use the local ranger will enforce camping time limits.

Water piped into picnic and campgrounds is safe to drink. Water from most free-moving streams at higher elevations is likewise safe to drink if it is reasonably free from all sources of contamination. Pools of sluggish or still water should not be used. When in doubt, boil water.

All birds and animals within the Forest are protected except for specific seasons on deer, bear and certain game birds. Especially protected are the bighorn sheep which can sometimes be sighted on high ridges of the taller peaks.

Certain areas of the Forest, sections of high ridges along the front country, near major highways, areas of habitation and recreation, are closed from July 1 until the first appreciable rainfall each year because of the danger of fire. About one-third of the Forest is thus closed annually.

A small portion of the San Gabriel Mountains is in the San Bernardino National Forest. This area is covered in the two sections of the book Chapters Ten and Eleven.

6

III ANGELES CREST HIGHWAY

Most scenic of all byways in the San Gabriel Mountains is this 56 mile drive which seeks out the best high country recreation sites from La Cañada to Big Pines.

Angeles Crest Highway. Main avenue of exploration into the San Gabriel Mountains is the Angeles Crest Highway, which starts in the foothill community of La Cañada, climbs the front country, etches a line into the higher elevations and ends, still in the mountains, at Big Pines.

The majority of the best high mountain picnic and camping sites lie along this highway—State Highway 2. From it you can drive to Mt. Wilson, into the historic West Fork of the San Gabriel River, out onto wind-whipped Blue Ridge, and down into the headwaters of the East Fork of the San Gabriel River in the Prairie Fork.

This is always a high speed highway, always at least two lanes wide, equipped with many turnouts and parking areas. Except during and after heavy snows it is kept open all year. Occasionally it is closed by snows and slides along its newest portion from Islip Saddle east to Vincent Saddle.

The first attempt to put a road into this country were the efforts of the Soledad Toll Road Company, some time around 1869. The scheme was abandoned when the Antelope Valley country became accessible by railroad.

From La Cañada the Angeles Crest Highway—built between 1929 and 1956 by depression day laborers, contract construction crews, and inmates—inches up the west wall of the Arroyo Seco, the canyon that serves as one of the water sources for the city of

7

Pasadena. From certain turnouts it is possible to look down into this deep canyon and see the Brown Canyon Debris Dam built by the Forest Service in 1942, the flat places that once held alder-shaded cabins before the 1938 flood. Badmen Juan Flores and Tiburcio Vasquez knew and used the Arroyo in their days.

The road passes the Angeles Crest ranger station, crosses the airy Woodwardia Canyon bridge, scene of the start of the disastrous Woodwardia fire that burned 14,000 acres here in October 1959, finally gains George's Gap, a saddle named after Abe George, one of the pioneer highway builders.

From George's Gap it is possible to look down into the drainage of Clear Creek, the Forest Service's tree plantation, the Clear Creek school camp operated by the Los Angeles City Schools, and beyond into the great trough of the Big Tujunga.

To the northeast the two prominent peaks, close at hand, are Josephine Peak, with the lookout tower on top; and Strawberry Peak.

The Crest Highway continues, in an easterly direction now, down to the intersection at Clear Creek with the Angeles Forest Highway, which leads north for 24 miles to Vincent on the edge of the Antelope Valley. (See Angeles Forest Highway, Chapter 13.)

From Clear Creek junction the Crest Highway drops briefly along the north side of the upper Arroyo Seco and climbs to the east.

Sideroad to Switzer's Camp. To the right here, is the well-marked partially-paved sideroad down into the Arroyo Seco for roughly a half mile to Switzer Campground and the historic old hiking way-point of Switzer's Camp. None of the old structures remain.

At the top of the Crest Highway's eastward climb here is Red Box, a saddle separating the Arroyo Seco and the West Fork of

*The road from Red Box up to Mt. Wilson is whittled
from solid rock walls.*

Snow is a sometimes visitor to the San Gabriel Mountains.

Photo by *Pasadena* Independent *Star-News*

the San Gabriel River. The place name comes from the historic box of fire fighting tools kept here that is painted red.

There is an Angeles National Forest ranger station here with an information desk, and here is the intersection with the Mt. Wilson Road.

Sideroad to Mt. Wilson. The Mt. Wilson Road was built in 1931-32 by the U.S. Bureau of Public Roads following the completion of the Angeles Crest Highway to Red Box. It provided a modern route to the complex of installations atop Mt. Wilson, supplanting the narrow, steep, unpaved Mt. Wilson Toll Road on the south face of the mountains.

This is a spectacular drive, carved from the north wall of a cluster of prominences that begin with San Gabriel Peak and range east through Occidental Peak out to the wooded point where Mt. Wilson stands.

Sideroad to Mt. Disappointment. Just south of the Red Box ranger station is a paved road that leads up via a series of easy switchbacks to the former Nike missile tracking site atop Mt. Disappointment. There are other Nike rocket and tracking sites in the San Gabriel range, some abandoned. All are closed to the public.

At a point three miles from Red Box along the Mt. Wilson Road is the Eaton Canyon Saddle, a turnout and a locked gate leading to the Forest Service truck trail down four miles to the site of the old Alpine Tavern terminus of the vanished Mt. Lowe Railway.

This truck trail is closed to vehicular traffic but the road provides an easy hike down to the Mt. Lowe Campground at the site of the old Alpine Tavern, whose rubbly walls were at last dynamited and cleared away in March of 1959. (See Mt. Lowe, Chapter 23.)

Past the Eaton Canyon Saddle the Mt. Wilson Road passes a

Photo by California Institute of Technology

Giant 100-inch Hooker telescope at Mt. Wilson.

metallic forest of radio and TV aerials and reaches the gate house of the Mt. Wilson property, admission 25 cents per person. Just to the right of the gate house is the gated entrance to the old Mt. Wilson Toll Road and trail which lead down to Sierra Madre and Altadena. (See Chapter 5.)

There is a resort here—the Mt. Wilson Hotel, 720 acres of private land—with a history that stretches back to Strain's Camp, circa 1889, and the building of the first hotel in the summer of 1905. This structure burned in 1913 and was rebuilt in 1915. It sees frequent visitors, and perhaps the most delighted of these are the children who are fascinated by the tamed wild songbirds here that will take crumbs from an outstretched hand. There are also tamed deer and squirrels.

Reached via a short, easy path from the Mt. Wilson Hotel parking lot is the famed Mt. Wilson telescope complex. Work on this 5,713-foot high astronomical outpost started in 1903 with surveys by Dr. George Ellery Hale of Yerkes Observatory. Operating today are the famed 100-inch Hooker telescope, completed in 1917; the 60-inch telescope, completed in 1909; and three solar telescopes, easily identifiable by the tall, silvery-white towers. Nearby is an exhibit hall of astronomical photographs. A visitors' gallery installed in the 100-inch telescope dome affords an opportunity to view the giant sky searcher. The telescopes are operated by the Carnegie Institution of Washington in cooperation with the California Institute of Technology.

Harvard University was first in the area with a telescope. It operated a 13-inch telescope on a site known as Signal Point about a half mile west of the Mt. Wilson Hotel from 1889 to 1890.

Sideroad to West Fork of the San Gabriel River. Just south of Red Box, on the left side, an unpaved, sometimes narrow, sometimes steep, frequently rough road leads down into the West Fork

12

country, and as far as conventional automobile travel is concerned, ends at the Forest Service's ranger station six miles distant.

This is a most pleasant drive in spring or early summer while the spring-fed West Fork is up and noisy. The road passes Camp Hi Hill, a part of the Long Beach City School system where sixth grade youngsters spend one week during their regular school year.

Camp Hi Hill was once Opid's Camp, founded in 1911 by Ludwik Opid and operated in later years by his son John. Opid's was one of the most famous of all the popular waystations in the mountain country during the great hiking era. It was near Opid's, in 1943, that twenty-six inches of rain fell in twenty-four hours, a Forest record.

When the road gains the canyon bottom, roughly three and a half miles from Red Box, the twin Valley Forge campgrounds —one for the public, one for pre-registered organizational and equestrian groups—are reached.

On some private land inholding along the road a few cabins can be seen.

The original West Fork ranger station is the oldest structure on the Angeles National Forest. It was built by rangers of the San Gabriel Timberland Reserve in 1900. It is said to be the first U.S. Forest Service ranger station built with government funds in the United States. The old log building, still solidly standing, will soon become a small forest museum.

From the public campgrounds here a gated truck trail reaches on into the West Fork of the San Gabriel River. A side road off this truck trail leads up past Spring Camp down the front side of the range into Monrovia. These roads are closed to the public but can be hiked in open season.

Angeles Crest Highway—resume. From Red Box the Crest

13

The Charlton Flat Picnic Area once called Pine Flats,
on the Angeles Crest Highway.

Just north of Chilao Campground is the store-restaurant
at Newcomb's.

Highway continues easterly now, finding its footing along the high north wall of the West Fork.

Sideroad to Barley Flats. An unpaved road that leads up the hill just east of Red Box climbs steeply to Barley Flats and the former Nike rocket launching site there. The buildings are now used as a county detention camp. The road is closed to vehicular traffic but may be hiked—except during the fire season closure. From Barley Flats a paved road runs east back down to the Crest Highway near Shortcut Saddle.

At the Shortcut Saddle the Crest Highway crosses the ridge separating the West Fork from the Upper Big Tujunga. From turnouts along here and at Shortcut Picnic Area it is possible now to look north and east deep into the high country of the San Gabriel Mountains. Here stand Mt. Waterman, 8038 feet; Twin Peaks, 7601 feet; Mt. Islip, 8260 feet; Throop Peak, 9134 feet; Mt. Hawkins, 8851 feet; Iron Mountain, 8028 feet; and Mt. Williamson, 8214 feet.

Roughly nine miles beyond Red Box is the beginning of the Charlton-Chilao Recreation Area. The first unit here is Charlton Flat, named after R. H. Charlton, former Angeles National Forest supervisor, the first day-use picnic ground in the Forest to utilize the metered pay-as-you-enter gate—50 cents per car per day. Here, too, is the Charlton Flat forest station with a showcase of historic and Indian lore from the area. Here is a nature trail.

There are 171 stoves and tables in this large, hill and canyon covering picnic ground complex, flush and pit toilets, piped water.

At Chilao, on the right side of the Crest Highway, a trail leads down into the roadless Devil's Canyon-Bear Canyon Wild Area, a bit of wilderness in the Angeles National Forest. There are a couple of trail camps in the preserve, trails are not maintained. Many people have been lost trying to hike through the area from top to bottom. It can be done, but only with difficulty. The Wild Area is the haunt of deer, bear, bobcat, mountain sheep, possibly mountain lion. The trail down from the Angeles Crest Highway is steep; coming back up it seems even steeper.

Two miles beyond Charlton Flat, past the blackened skeleton of burnt trees on the north side, scene of the 1954 85-acre Charlton Fire; past the Forest Service lookout atop pyramidal Vetter Mountain, is Chilao Campground, one of the largest in the Angeles National Forest, 150 camping units plus Willow Trailer Campground.

In a grove of Jeffrey pine, Coulter pine, incense cedar and big cone Douglas fir, Chilao is enormously popular with Southland campers and picnickers. Weekends in the summertime frequently find it, and other camps along the Angeles Crest Highway, filled. Just beyond Chilao on the Crest Highway is the store-restaurant at Newcomb's where a limited variety of supplies is available. Opposite the store is the historic Newcomb homestead where Louie Newcomb built his first cabin in 1890.

Sideroad to Loomis Ranch, Mt. Pacifico, Pinyon Flats. From the Chilao Campground complex—there is a ranger station, ranger residence, hotshot fire crew camp and heliport here—an unpaved road leads west into the drainage of Alder Creek and looks down into that great bowl. Here a gated and locked road leads down to the historic old Loomis Ranch, hewed out of the mountain wilderness in 1913 by Captain (of Los Angeles police) Lester G. Loomis and his wife Grace—it was the last homestead to be patented in the Angeles National Forest. For years it was a popular stopping point for mountain hikers. In more recent years the ranch has served as an organization camp, and has sat abandoned. The historic apple orchard—from which Mrs. Loomis once made apple

16

dumplings that drew rhapsodies of praise from hikers—has grown wild.

Beyond the locked Loomis Ranch turnoff the dirt road continues north to a junction with a loop road back to the Crest Highway via Horse Flats (a large and slightly lesser-used Forest Service campground, suitable for trailers), Bandido Group Camp (on a reservation basis only for organizations and horseback riding groups), and a scattering of private organizational camps including Cumorah Crest, Singing Pines, Christian Camp, Hidden Valley and Rosenita.

Past this junction our dirt road continues north to another fork. Here the right hand road leads to Pinyon Flats, Sulphur Springs Campground (eight units) and down the hill into Little Rock Creek and on out to Little Rock Reservoir and Campground. (See Little Rock Reservoir, Chapter 12.) The left hand byway leads across the south face of Mt. Pacifico to two campgrounds, one in the saddle and one at the summit at the end of a spur road. (There are eight units here altogether.) Past Pacifico this byway runs on west, finally zigzags down the west face of Round Top into Mill Creek Summit ranger station on the Angeles Forest Highway. (See Angeles Forest Highway, Chapter 13.)

Angeles Crest Highway—resume. The Angeles Crest Highway gets in some of its climbing here beyond Chilao, laboring without effort along the north side of Mt. Waterman. The ridge off to the north that is burned over is the result of the 1953 Sulphur Fire that consumed 32,635 acres of high value watershed and timber.

Just opposite the road back down to Bandito and Horse Flats, on the right hand side of the Crest Highway, is the start of a new trail which runs for seven miles to Twin Peaks Saddle, and on to Mt. Waterman.

Most of the small dirt roads that branch off the highway along this stretch are logging roads, part of the sanitation-salvage logging operation conducted by the Forest in 1960 and 1961. Although unmarked, they are generally closed to motor vehicles but are open to hikers.

Private organization camps are passed: Valcrest, Camp Glenwood, Camp Pajarito. Then the road gains Cloudburst Summit, 7,018 feet, until the opening of the last section of the Crest Highway, the highest point along its run.

Sideroad to Cooper Canyon Campground. Off to the left here is a one and a half mile unpaved road leading back to the pleasant Cooper Canyon Campground, four units, but with considerable area for development. The road is closed to auto traffic.

Angeles Crest Highway now passes two ski areas.

The first is Mt. Waterman, its chair lift being the first on the Forest, built in 1941. The lift is 2,100 feet long, frequently runs on weekends in warm weather for sight-seers. There are adjacent rope tows and ski runs, warming hut and lunch facilities. Ski rentals are available at Newcomb's.

Sideroad to Buckhorn Campground. The unpaved road on the left here reaches down into a tributary of Cooper Canyon to Buckhorn Campground, thirty-five units plus trailer spaces. There are some permanent mortars in the large stones here, proof of Indian occupation. A trail opposite Buckhorn forest station leads to the top of Mt. Waterman.

On the right side of the Crest Highway we come to the second area ski resort: Kratka Ridge. Here is an 1,800-foot chair lift, built in 1953, with rope tows, warming hut, lunch facilities, ski rentals.

Past Kratka Ridge the Crest Highway reaches Vista Picnic area —twelve units—situated in a small saddle on Kratka Ridge. From

One of the tunnels on the Angeles Crest Highway through the cliffs of Mt. Williamson. Bighorn sheep have been seen on hill above tunnel.

the picnic site a fine view of the Bear Canyon country to the south is offered.

Just beyond Vista is Ridge Crest Picnic Area—seven units—and then a large overlook into Bear Canyon. This was once the end of the road and beyond you'll find the remains of the old inmate camp, Camp 37, which is being razed to make way for a new, large picnic area.

Past old Camp 37 the Crest Highway winds on east, passing through the two tunnels at Mt. Williamson—named after Lieutenant Robert Stockton Williamson who conducted a railroad survey along the desert side of the area in 1854—and reaching the junction with State Highway 39, the Crystal Lake Spur. Bighorn sheep have been seen on the rocky walls between the two tunnels, usually very early in the morning.

Sideroad to Crystal Lake, and the San Gabriel River country. A new, wide, paved highway turns right here, travels along the west side of Mt. Islip above Bear Canyon. This road reaches Crystal Lake and continues south into the San Gabriel River drainage and on to Azusa. (See San Gabriel Canyon, Chapter 7.)

Past Islip Saddle the Crest Highway passes Pine Hollow picnic area on the left—seventeen units.

Sideroad to Little Jimmy Campground. The new dirt road that turns off to the right here is closed to auto traffic, but can be hiked up the north face of Mt. Islip approximately one and a half miles to one of the most attractive of the Forest's smaller high country sites. Beyond is the trail to Little Jimmy Springs, Windy Gap—one half mile away—and then on to Throop Peak, Mt. Baden-Powell—six miles—which crests at 9,399 feet. The trail then zigzags down the north face of Mt. Baden-Powell to Vincent Gap on the Crest Highway.

Past the Little Jimmy turnoff the Crest Highway reaches Dawson, Saddle, highest point of the entire run of highway—7,980 feet. There are several spectacular views of the Antelope Valley, Mojave Desert country from turnouts here. A variety of forest trees and shrubs grow in this higher elevation. Here is the home of the chinquipin, and ground cover of white thorn and manzanita. Lodgepole pine can be spotted along the highway, as can white fir and limber pine. Here is Jeffrey pine, ponderosa pine, sugar pine.

Two smaller picnic areas are passed: Lodge Pole, eight units, and White Thorn, ten units.

The Crest Highway in this area passes a pair of side canyons reaching down from Mt. Baden-Powell where frequently old snow —melted and refrozen into ice—stands all summer. Always shaded, and chilly at these upper elevations, the two ravines of ice are frequently referred to by hiking groups and Scouters as "the glaciers," although actually they are no such thing.

At Vincent Gap stands the large Forest Service sign pointing the way to the Mt. Baden-Powell trail. The peak was named on May 30, 1931, in honor of Lord Baden-Powell, founder of the Boy Scout movement. A memorial marker stands at the summit of the peak and annual pilgrimages are conducted by Southland Boy Scouts to the peak's summit.

Along the summit ridge of Mt. Baden-Powell stands the Ancient Limber Pine Forest, a grove of weather-tortured trees discovered by Angeles Forest Supervisor Sim Jarvi in 1962 to be 1,000 to 2,000 years old. One of the pines, the Waldron Tree, stands in honor of Michael H. "Wally" Waldron, volunteer Scouter who organized much of the Scouts' homage to the mountain peak.

From Vincent Gap, too, to the right, is the trail to the old Big Horn Mine, situated around the bulk of Mt. Baden-Powell and some three miles distant.

An excellent view of the upper end of the drainage of the East

Fork of the San Gabriel River can be had from Vincent Gap: Prairie Fork, Fish Fork stand out clearly as do the peaks behind such as Pine Mountain, Iron Mountain, and capping them all, Mount San Antonio (Old Baldy), highest in the range at 10,064 feet.

Sideroad into Big Rock Creek. To the left here an unpaved road runs down into Big Rock Creek to Big Rock Campground, elevation 5,500 feet, ten units; Paradise Springs; South Fork Campground, elevation 4,500 feet, fifteen units; and Sycamore Flats, elevation 4,200 feet, twelve units. The road becomes paved just above the turnoff into South Fork. And from South Fork Campground you can gain the Devil's Punchbowl via a two-mile trail. This sunken, giant rock-flanked area sits adjacent to the San Andreas Fault and reflects some of that geological feature's capriciousness. The site has been made into a Los Angeles County park.

Sideroad to Jackson Flat area. An unpaved road also takes off to the left here and climbs the corner of Blue Ridge north of the Angeles Crest Highway and runs through Jackson Flat into Grassy Hollow Campground back, on a loop, at the Crest Highway.

Past Vincent Gap the Angeles Crest Highway swings in a sweeping curve, past Inspiration Point, and then gains a summit on Blue Ridge of 7,386 feet. To the left here is Grassy Hollow Campground—fourteen units.

Sideroad to Blue Ridge, and the Prairie Fork country. An unpaved side road turns off to the right here and follows Blue Ridge out to a campground bearing its name—ten units—then runs on to Guffy Campground, ten units. Beyond Guffy the dirt road drops via switchbacks steeply down through pleasant timbered country in the Prairie Fork and runs down that watercourse to Lupin Campground and past the Prairie Fork Forest Station to the end of the road at Cabin Flat Campground.

From here it is possible for the experienced hiker to follow the rough trail down the Prairie Fork to the junction with Vincent Gulch and Mine Gulch, then on past Iron Fork down the East Fork of the San Gabriel River to reunion with pavement at the Cattle Canyon ranger station. The distance is roughly sixteen miles, and it is a rugged hike with many fords, many scrambles over rocks. It is not a recommended easy one-day hike for novices.

Angeles Crest Highway—resume. From the Blue Ridge spine the Crest Highway descends now into Big Pines and at the poplar-shaded junction with the Wrightwood to Valyermo Road, the Angeles Crest Highway ends. Many folks consider, however, that the Angeles Crest Highway runs through Big Pines and Wrightwood, past Mountain Top and the junction with State Highway 138, down West Cajon all the way to U.S. Highway 66 at Cajon.

Sideroad to old Big Pines Campground. An unpaved side road leads off to the southwest here, climbing back up Blue Ridge on another tack, touching many scattered camping and picnicking sites. Here are Shady Slope Campground and Knob Picnic Area. In the Big Pines Campground complex there are forty-six picnic units, room for trailers and piped water.

Adjacent is the Blue Ridge ski area, with a double and single chair lift, warming huts, lunch facilities, ski instruction and rentals.

(For other campgrounds and recreation facilities in the Big Pines area see Cajon to Valyermo, Chapter 11.)

IV ARROYO SECO

The road up the Arroyo Seco above Pasadena is closed to motor vehicles, but a walk up this pleasant canyon will recall the era when summer cabins and hikers dominated the foothill country.

Arroyo Seco. At the intersection of Windsor Avenue and Ventura Street in Altadena is a locked gate across a road leading back up the Arroyo Seco. At one time this paved road was open to the public all the way up canyon to Oakwilde. This was prior to the 1938 flood. The way station of Oakwilde was a jumping off place for hikes to Switzer's Camp and beyond. Since the damaging flood, the City of Pasadena Water Department has closed the road to vehicular traffic. The construction of the Brown Canyon Debris Dam has helped to wipe out traces of the road into Oakwilde. The many cabins that once dotted the canyon have been razed and only the picturesque foundations and cobbled walks and walls stand to remind the hiker or horseback rider of the more peaceful days when this was Pasadena's most pleasant Sunday outing site.

Still by spring it is a delightful spot, although flood and flood controllers have removed much of the lush green water-seeking willow, sycamore, alder and bay that grew along the canyon bottom. The road, with its many fords and few rickety bridges, is especially popular with equestrians.

24

V MOUNT WILSON ROAD

Up from Altadena this former toll road climbs; it knew the shake splitters of Don Benito Wilson's day, and the moving up the hill of the parts of the great observatory.

Henniger Flats, Mount Wilson Toll Road. According to historians, it was Benjamin Davis (Don Benito) Wilson who ordered the building of the first trail up from the Sierra Madre area to Mt. Wilson in 1864. Wilson was after lumber—fence posts, shakes and staves for wine barrels.

By 1899 A. G. Strain had built his camp atop the summit of Mt. Wilson and shortly thereafter came the scientists making the astronomical tests. As a result of the increased traffic up the hill, via Wilson Trail and another, rougher trail up Eaton Canyon (then called Precipicio or Precipice Canyon), the Mount Wilson Toll Road Company was formed on August 7, 1889. While it was the goal of this group to build a road, first they worked on the trail, widening it to six feet. Later came the further cliff clawing that widened the path to ten feet which would see the upward hauling of the 60-inch and 100-inch telescope equipment. In its day, hundreds of thousands of passengers rode stage and automobiles up this track safely.

Today the dirt road that jumps off from Pinecrest Drive in Altadena—gated and locked—leads up to the Los Angeles County's Forest Nursery at Henniger Flats—named after a homesteader in the area, William K. Henniger—and then with zigzags and narrow cliff hanging passages, gains Mt. Wilson summit just west of the gatehouse to the Mt. Wilson Hotel Co. property.

While it is closed to public automobiles, jeeps and motorcycles, it is a fine hike during the spring and snowless winter days. It is 10 miles from top to bottom. It is a better downhill hike and many groups are ferried to the top, dumped off, and hike down to Alta-dena. There is no water along the route except at Henniger Flats.

VI CHANTRY FLATS ROAD— BIG SANTA ANITA

An avenue above Arcadia that leads back to one of the favorite jumping off places for hikes into the Big Santa Anita Canyon and mountain country beyond.

Chantry Flats, Big Santa Anita Canyon. Santa Anita Avenue runs north through Arcadia and when it hits the foothills it becomes Santa Anita Canyon Road. It leads back 3.5 miles past the Santa Anita Dam, on a road that was first scratched through between 1931-1935, to CCC-constructed Chantry Flats, a Forest Service picnic area, ranger station, pack station and restaurant, and the jumping off place for hiking in the colorful Big Santa Anita Canyon.

Chantry Flats, named after a yesterday miner, C. E. Chantry, who used to drive a diminutive burro up the old Big Santa Anita trail all the way to Chilao where he had gold prospects, is another of the mountains' most heavily used picnic areas—thirty units, no overnight camping. Here is stationed Bill Adams' string of mules, burros and horses used in packing supplies down into the canyon for the occupants of the ninety-odd cabins strung along the stream. Adams' colorful pack string is the only one in the San Gabriel Mountains, and can be seen almost daily making the trip down the switchbacked canyon trail hauling in food, fuel, luggage for cabin dwellers and visitors at the Methodist camp at Sturtevant's.

The Big Santa Anita Canyon trail is one of the most heavily used in the Angeles National Forest. Weekends may see as many as 600 hikers on the track that leads from Chantry Flats down into the canyon bottom, then up the watercourse past the scars of historic Roberts Camp and Fern Lodge, past Sturtevant Falls,

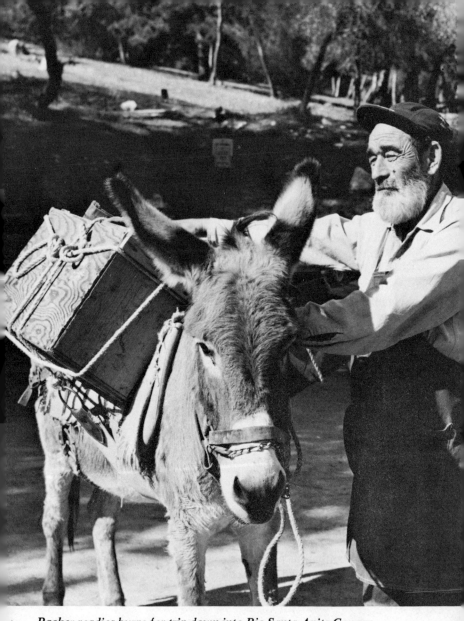

Packer readies burro for trip down into Big Santa Anita Canyon cabin area.

Spruce Grove trail campground with eight family units, the Cascades and on to Sturtevant's Camp. Another canyon bottom trail reaches up Winter Creek past many cabins and historic Hoegee's Camp, recently converted from a special use camp into a new trail campground with fifteen family units. The new campground fittingly is called Hoegee's.

At Sturtevant's Camp, the main canyon bottom trail forks; one leg leads up to Mt. Wilson, and the other finds Newcomb's Pass (Arthur Carter, Louis Newcomb and John Hartwell built trail in the old days, according to Sierra Madre historian Bill Wark), drops down into the West Fork of the San Gabriel River and from here leads, via Shortcut Canyon, to Charlton Flats, Chilao and the high country beyond.

The old canyon trail of Chantry's day was routed differently along the lower end. It started in Sierra Madre, climbed over the ridge to upper Winter Creek, dropped from there into Sturtevant's Camp. The canyon bottom trail was built between 1910-1911.

Water runs in the Big Santa Anita Canyon streambed year around, and becomes boisterous at times during and after heavy rains. In rainy weather or drought, veteran canyon dwellers still pronounce it the most pleasant place to live in the San Gabriel Mountains.

VII SAN GABRIEL CANYON ROAD

A gold rush, a flood-destroyed mining community, a bridge that goes nowhere, Crystal Lake, these are some of the interesting points of history and scenery up this byway out of Azusa.

San Gabriel Canyon. Of all the canyons that cut the chaparraled San Gabriel Mountains, this one is the most storied; here emanate more stories, more legends, more color than the rest of the range.

The quest for gold has written most of this excitement: the boom, the badmen, murders, a town washed away by flood. Still the canyon holds other colorful features. Here the U.S. Navy tests weapons of the future. Here is an avenue into the Devil's Canyon-Bear Canyon Wild Area, the only roadless preserve of its kind within the Angeles National Forest. Indians lived here and left their mark. A stage line once ran up the old canyon road, and the new highway leads up to the Crystal Lake complex, a popular and unusually scenic camping area.

From Azusa the San Gabriel Canyon Road runs north. The San Gabriel Canyon, with its West, North and East Forks, is one of the principal watershed drainages of the mountain range, and the scars at the mouth of the stream hint of early day flooding when walls of boulder-carrying water hammered down the course into the San Gabriel Valley.

At a sideroad in the mouth of the canyon, the resort of El Encanto is reached, and beyond, on this same road, the lower canyon bottom is explored via this older canyon road. An old railroad tunnel stands near the end of this deadend road, evidence of dam construction work on the Morris Dam in the 1930s.

Photo by U.S. Navy

*Variable angle torpedo launcher at U.S. Navy installation
at Morris Dam in San Gabriel River above Azusa.*

The Morris Dam is the first landmark along the San Gabriel Canyon Road. Named after engineer Samuel B. Morris, the Morris or Pine Canyon Dam was built between 1932 and 1934 for the City of Pasadena. The structure, 756 feet wide at the top, and 245 feet high, is designed to hold back 42,000 acre feet of water in a canyon bottom reservoir four miles long.

It was in September of 1943 that the placid mountain pond was taken over by Caltech for torpedo testing, and so practical did this prove that the Navy established a permanent facility there, in conjunction with its Pasadena Naval Ordnance Test Station, in October of 1945. The great machinery of the variable angle torpedo launcher dominates the landscape at the reservoir.

Cabins, old road, abandoned little orchards stand beneath the highwater mark of the lake here.

Almost at the end of the four-mile lake behind Morris Dam are the scars where earthmoving machines gouged out the fill for the great stone and earthen dam of San Gabriel Dam No. 1 on up canyon. The water behind this barrier, built in 1938, backs up as far as the East Fork bridge, another four miles. The dam is 1,520 feet long, 320 feet high, holds back 43,825 acre feet of water.

There are informal access roads down from the highway to lake side here, and fishing is allowed in this sometimes pond.

Sideroad into East Fork of the San Gabriel River. A good paved road crosses a bridge here, runs east along one of the principal tributaries of the stream back into the lower East Fork.

This is the most historic corner of the San Gabriel River country. Gold was discovered in the East Fork in 1855. The precious metal was found in placers here, and early prospectors could pan as much as $6 and $7 a day from the stream.

The Santa Anita Mining Co. was organized in 1859 and that

year the mining camp of Eldoradoville came up. Probably a tent camp, it was big enough, and permanent enough, that in the election of 1860 400 votes were cast from Eldoradoville for Abraham Lincoln. The town had three general stores, half a dozen saloons and dance halls, according to canyon historian Sedley Peck. It was located at the junction of Cattle Canyon and the East Fork.

Damaged in its first year by high water, the town was completely erased by flood in 1862; nothing remained. According to the best information, no sketch or photograph of the camp has survived.

Hydraulic mining was employed in the East Fork with H. C. Roberts and William G. Fergusson racing to see who could first bring ditch water down canyon for the monitors. A keen eye can still find some of the ditch scars along the canyon walls. The hydraulic adventure was not successful, and state laws eventually forced its abandonment.

A colorful crew lived along the East Fork in the old days: George Trogden, whose mail and supply cabin stood at Iron Fork and who was buried there; "Twitchlip" Kelly, Peg Leg Bill Coynes, Old Man Armstrong, Uncle Jimmy Grayson, One-Eyed Mountain Charlie, Soldier Thompson and Two-Gun Don Kosenkrantz, they of the colorful names; Oliver Justice, who was buried in a coffin he had hand-hewn himself in his pre-dug grave above Iron Fork; John Robb, who sluiced gold from sawdust swept from the saloon floors of Eldoradoville.

Before the flood of 1938 a paved road ran up the East Fork all the way to the Narrows. The flood chewed this avenue to pieces in a random spree of destruction. Still standing, intact but going nowhere, is a highway bridge near the Narrows. No road meets the bridge at either end; those bits of pavement were washed away by the flood.

Near the point where the sideroad of the Glendora Mountain

33

Photo by U.S. Forest Service

*Fishing—and gold panning—are popular sports in the
East Fork of the San Gabriel River.*

Road runs down from its high course into the canyon, the East Fork stream is shaded by a thicket of cottonwoods and sycamores. Here, on almost every weekend, you'll find amateur gold panners at work, sometimes getting a fleck or two to tweezer into a pill bottle of water for "show." Even the more serious miners with sluice claims farther up the canyon never take out much more than this, only colors.

There is a store and restaurant at Williams Camp in the East Fork, and the Oaks Picnic Area, near the junction of the Glendora Mountain Road, provides a handful of picnic tables and stoves.

A great high sideroad takes off to the north from the canyon bottom. Designed originally to pierce the building ridges above the northward running East Fork via a series of tunnels, this road was destined to follow the East Fork all the way to Vincent Gap. Plans now indicate that a fork of the inmate-constructed road will curve back to the west and will afford passage into the Bichota Canyon country with eventual end at the San Gabriel Canyon Road between Rincon and Coldbrook.

Hiking up the East Fork is pleasant and interesting. The road ends at the new Forest Station near Cattle Canyon, called the East Fork station. (See Chapter 3.)

Back on the main San Gabriel Canyon Road, the avenue points on north, reaches Rincon. Here, across the stream from the resort on the eastern edge of the stream, stands a large boulder, house-sized, that still bears faded traces of Indian pictograph writing on its western face. Years ago, when the writing was plainer, it was photographed and studied by experts. Their opinion: the many tally marks were probably game counts. Most pictograph rocks stand along or near game trails.

Rincon, a historic site in the canyon, is soon to be made into a park. A forest station stands here.

Just beyond the Rincon site is the closed sideroad into the West

Fork of the San Gabriel River. While the road is barred to vehicular traffic, it can be hiked, and it is a popular area with fishermen. Back along this avenue, too, is the trail into the bottom of the Devil's Canyon-Bear Canyon Wild Area. Cogswell Dam lies up this byway. This road goes through to the Upper West Fork country on the north side of Mt. Wilson, but the down-canyon road is open to auto traffic only as far as the West Fork forest station most of the season.

The North Fork of the San Gabriel River is the course the road follows now, and here it is tree-shaded and most attractive.

Coldbrook, with its forest station and Forest Service campground, is a historic spot. Squirrel Inn once stood here in the old days, with a popular waitress at the inn named Nellie Hawkins. Her charm prompted the naming of nearby Mt. Hawkins in her honor according to one mountain legend.

On up the hill the road climbs now. Turnouts provide vistas of the lower reaches of the canyon and the higher peaks that flank the watercourse: Mt. Hawkins, South Mt. Hawkins, to the east; Smith Mountain and the Twin Peaks country to the west. Here, just below Crystal Lake, tucked away in a green and well-watered canyon, is the Falling Springs resort; a restaurant, lodge, attractive cabins, a small store. Delightful by deep summer when much of the surrounding area is dry, Falling Springs will be damp and verdant.

Sideroad to the Angeles Crest Highway. At the entrance to the Crystal Lake area is the new sideroad, the Crystal Lake spur, leading to the west around the bulk of Mt. Islip to the Angeles Crest Highway at Islip Saddle. (See Chapter 3.)

Crystal Lake is another one of the show places of the Angeles National Forest. The lake, usually low and seldom handsome, is popular with fishermen if not with aesthetes. There is a small bait shop, store, restaurant at the lake.

Much more imposing is the vast Crystal Lake Campground, with 250 family units. This area is frequently filled to overflowing in season, with both individual families and Scout troops and other organizations camping among the giant pines.

There is a store here, where campers may buy supplies. The Forest Service has provided a visitor information service program and a nature trail in the area. The campground facilities are modern, if taxed during summer weekends. A system of hiking trails radiate back from Crystal Lake to sites like Little Jimmy Springs, Mt. South Hawkins, and the Windy Gap, Lily Springs country.

There is a forest station at Crystal Lake.

VIII GLENDORA MOUNTAIN ROAD

Above Glendora is this winding avenue that offers many impressive views of valley and deep mountains. It ends at Mt. Baldy Village.

Glendora Mountain Road, Glendora Ridge Road. Affording by winter, when snow is on the high country, some of the most spectacular views in the mountain region, is the joined Glendora Mountain Road-Glendora Ridge Road.

Built in the early 1930s, the Glendora Mountain Road, a paved, high-speed though frequently curved mountain byway, starts in Glendora at the end of eastward running Sierra Madre Avenue.

A short distance beyond the road's beginning is the Dalton Forest station; the sideroad, back up Big Dalton Canyon, now closed to the public; and Little Dalton Campground, twelve units.

Then the road climbs the front country, first offering views of the San Gabriel Valley from various turnouts, and later, as it reaches more altitude, a view down into the San Dimas Experiment Station, completely burned out by fire in 1960.

The Glendora Mountain Road actually ends when it reaches a fork and then runs down the hill to the East Fork of the San Gabriel Canyon. At this fork the Glendora Ridge Road begins and it runs on north and east, now offering some spectacular views of deep Cattle and Cow Canyon country off the East Fork, and finally Coldwater Canyon and a frontal view of Mount San Antonio, Old Baldy Peak.

The Glendora Ridge Road finally terminates at the Mt. Baldy Road right at the edge of Mt. Baldy Village.

IX MT. BALDY ROAD

From the Claremont-Upland area the twin Mt. Baldy roads open a scenic resort area with a history of gold mining. There is a fine ski area almost atop the range's tallest peak.

San Antonio Canyon, Mt. Baldy country. The lure of gold was always strong in the San Gabriel Mountains. There were minor booms at half a dozen places: near Acton, up along Mill Creek, in the East Fork of the San Gabriel River, on the side of Mt. Baden-Powell, in Lytle Creek and in this canyon, San Antonio.

Under ordinary circumstances the small amounts of gold seen in streams might have been overlooked, but forty to fifty years after the big boom in the Mother Lode prospectors were still hoping to hit the big bonanza in California. They had to look everywhere.

It was mining operations in Lytle Creek, the next major canyon complex east of San Antonio, that first led to miners poking over Lytle Creek Divide down into the upper San Antonio.

After that, date undetermined, a trail was built, which was followed by a wagon road around 1893 up the canyon. Later, after a heroic battle between Charles N. Baynham and the San Antonio Water Co. over canyon right-of-way, a toll road was built and lasted until 1922. Then the road was purchased by San Bernardino and Los Angeles counties and made into a public thoroughfare.

Today there are actually two roads up San Antonio Canyon: the old or the lower road, and the new or the upper road.

The old road has its history rooted in the early days when the route evolved from trail to wagon road to toll road. The upper road, straighter and with less-abrupt grades, was built in 1955.

The older road may be reached by driving north from the Ontario-Upland area on Euclid Avenue, the pepper tree-planted double drive.

At the head of Euclid Avenue the Mt. Baldy road bends to the west, passes the earthen dam built by the U.S. Army Corps of Engineers in 1956, passes orange orchards, an orchid nursery and gains a junction in the road.

Here at the Lower San Antonio Forest Station, is a spur road leading to the new, upper road. Up the canyon bottom the road is more meandering, passes small organizational camps, offers glimpses of the sycamore, laurel, alder shaded, boulder-strewn stream. Golden cup oak grows here.

Then the natural barrier of The Hogback is reached; the old road climbs stiffly and runs into the upper highway.

Sideroad to Glendora Ridge Road. (See Chapter 8.)

A short distance beyond, past an historic area known as the Strawberry Patch, Mt. Baldy Village is gained. Here is the area ranger station, a cluster of homes that knows a permanent year-around population of 300 residents, a church, a fire department, post office and a school—kindergarten to the eighth grade, with 75 students. From here on up the hill there are a number of stores, resorts, restaurants, that have come up since the historic Dell's Camp of the earliest days. These include Mt. Baldy Lodge, Buck-horn Restaurant, Mt. Baldy Park, Ice House Canyon Resort, and Snow Crest Resort.

The elevation at Mt. Baldy Village is 4,200 feet. As you move on up canyon the road climbs steadily. Ice House Resort is 5,000 feet, and the road switchbacks up in earnest as it climbs, passes the Forest Service's Glacier Campground, 5,500 feet.

Snow Crest Resort stands at 6,200 feet elevation, Manker Flats

Campground, named after pioneer canyon dweller Fletcher Manker, is 6,300 feet, and then the road ends at the parking area for the Mt. Baldy Ski Lift.

The main Mt. Baldy chair lift runs from the parking area, 6,500 feet, to the Notch, 7,800 feet. This lift operates daily in snow season and on weekends during the summer.

At the Notch the resort has a restaurant-lodge, and nearby is a rental building where skis, boots, poles, etc., can be rented. By summer there is straw to ski on here; winter usually provides snow.

Two more double chair lifts reach for higher altitudes from the Notch into the Thunder Mountain region. There is a trail out toward the Devil's Backbone, a sometimes spooky but always fascinating trek to the very summit of Mt. Baldy or Old Baldy. Its correct name is Mount San Antonio, highest peak in the San Gabriel Mountains. Its most recent altitude, from the U.S. Geological Survey, is 10,064 feet.

For the inexperienced hiker, there are some steep dropoffs in the area to be wary of. Most of these have been signed, but in spite of such warning, there have been several fatalities in recent years where hikers and sight-seers walked too close to the edge of these steep precipices, lost their footing and fell. Such spots are particularly hazardous in icy weather.

On the way down the hill there are two points of interest that are missed coming up the lower road. One, just past the old road junction, is the grave of Jacob Shinner, born 1827, died in a mining accident in the canyon in 1877. A turnout and a steep road up a slight hill to the grave is on the right side of the road.

Beyond, in a turnout on the left or canyon side of the upper road, is the historical monument calling attention to the site of the first hydraulic power plant in California, built in San Antonio Canyon in 1892, which, using transformers supplied by George Westinghouse, supplied electricity to the Pomona area.

The upper road gains Foothill Boulevard just east of Claremont via Padua Avenue or Mills Avenue.

The San Antonio Canyon country is filled with stories and legends. Apocryphal is the only label for the story of a search for a landslide-buried mining era saloon which a prospector is reported to have fallen into recently. Inside the ancient saloon the hiker reported finding intact glassware and still palatable liquor.

There are many handsome big conifers in the canyon. Ask at the Mt. Baldy Village ranger station as to the location of the Old Glory, near cabin 21, a heroic-proportioned big cone Douglas fir.

Up Cedar Canyon, above Ice House Resort, a giant cedar with an eleven-foot girth draws comments. This canyon is also the route to Cucamonga Peak and the Cucamonga Wild Area.

Gold mining, the activity that opened the rugged, cool, mountain canyon, flourished in the upper reaches from 1862, with James S. Banks making the original find.

After that there was a spread of activity that covered a sprawling section of the high country. By 1900 the bloom was rubbed off San Antonio mining. F. H. Manker, canyon historian, noted: "It has cost thousands of dollars to find out that mining in San Antonio Canyon does not pay."

In recent years mining activity has been mainly of the weekend-prospector type. Resort living and the summit snow activities keep the canyon busy today.

X LYTLE CREEK ROAD

In the San Bernardino National Forest, north out of Fontana, is this picturesque drive back to a resort area, the site of gold and timber prospecting, and pleasant campgrounds.

Lytle Creek. Outside the Angeles National Forest but still within the geographical confines of the San Gabriel Mountains is this pleasant avenue into the mountain country.

Sierra Avenue runs north of Fontana and Foothill Boulevard past the Devore Cutoff road into the mouth of Lytle Creek, part of the drainage of the Santa Ana River.

Shortly past the Devore Road the canyon changes its appearance from a broad streambed to a more confined canyon.

It was near this mouth of the canyon that Captain Andrew Lytle, commanding one of three Mormon companies from Utah, camped in 1851. Among the first settlers were the Wixom Brothers, Dave H. and Willard, around 1857. Silas Glenn and his family settled in the canyon in 1867.

According to historian Will Thrall gold was first discovered in the canyon in the 1860s. Fortunate miners made $40 a day from the gravels along the stream. In 1890 it was reported that about 100 miners were in the canyon, working their rockers and Long Toms, making around $4 per day. James S. Banks located mining properties high in the saddle between Lytle Creek and San Antonio Canyon, saw the birth of the famed Hocumac Mine and the subsequent activity. Most mining operations in the canyon ended in 1891 with the flood that February. Desultory placering operations took place until the 1930s, but as it was mostly beans and potatoes mining, no one made a fortune at the work.

43

From the mouth of the narrow canyon, the Lytle Creek road passes the San Sevaine truck trail, enters the San Bernardino National Forest. Here is the easterly approach to the Cucamonga Wild Area.

Fire scars stand along here, for the lower canyon has known two wind-whipped blazes in years past. The road crosses a bridge and the canyon, first on the right, is now on the left of the road.

Here and there a big cone Douglas fir puts in an appearance on the side mountains. Canyon live oak is more plentiful.

Right along the road, a mine tunnel yawns. Here is the dirt sideroad to the Lytle Creek Divide, and here is a Penny Pines plantation.

The Lytle Creek District Ranger Station (Cajon District of the San Bernardino National Forest, Star Route, Box 100, Fontana, California) stands on a great tree-shaded flat, once an Indian site. The cluster of residences, shops and station buildings is hidden from the road by a grove of conifers, a most attractive setting.

Beyond, past the Green Mountain Ranch resort, the stream begins to take on its most attractive form. Sycamore, alder and willow grow densely along the course of running water.

The small canyon settlement with the post office at the Happy Jack Trading Post stands here. The canyon has a permanent population of around 425 persons.

The canyon-following Applewhite Campground and picnic area now contains thirty-five picnic units, thirty-five camping sites. It is a pleasant region, particularly those units along the tree-shaded, bubbling stream.

The resorts of Scotland Store, Call of the Canyon and Dunham's Store stand here; the historic Glenn Ranch property is passed.

There is a sideroad here near the Applewhite Campground that leads east to the Barstow Freeway and Blue Cut in the Cajon country.

The tree-shaded ranger station at Lytle Creek.

Here the paved road ends. Beyond a rough, chuckholed, rubbly, unpaved byway leads back to Stockton Flat, elevation 5,500 feet and in a handsome timbered setting at the head of Lytle Creek. There is a Forest Service campground here, nine family units, and a pair of sideroads take off from this spot. One leads up over Lytle Creek Ridge into Lone Pine Canyon; the second reaches steeply up for Baldy Notch. The latter is not a through road and is hazardous in the wintertime because of ice at the higher elevations. Neither unpaved avenue should be attempted right after bad storms or snowfalls.

Stockton Flat lies in a sloping bowl ringed by high peaks and ridges. In spite of the rough road leading into the site, it is quite busy by summer. In the winter it can be chilly and windy. Spring finds the road in sad repair, but the countryside fresh and handsome.

Lytle Creek, with its history of Indian encampments, a gold boom, timber claims, the Glenns, the Applewhites, Happy Jack Joseph Pollard, the floods and the constant rebirth of beauty up the canyon, is fairest because of its barren appearance at the canyon mouth. Many-forked, with a stream that knows ten thousand attractive shade trees on its run past the Glenn Ranch, Lytle Creek is one of the lesser-known, more enchanting canyons in the San Gabriel Mountains.

XI CAJON TO VALYERMO ROAD

From the Cajon Pass country this byway runs through Wrightwood, the Big Pines Recreation Area, all the way to the Mojave Desert region near Valyermo.

Cajon Junction to Valyermo. Slicing along the east edge of the San Gabriel Range is State Highway 138 and a network of fine mountain roads that run through Swarthout Valley, Wrightwood, the Big Pines area, down along Pinyon Ridge into Valyermo.

Few byways in the San Gabriel Mountains will show such a diversity of terrain and flora: the latter ranges from the Joshua trees of the desert levels, to the great patriarchal pines atop Table Mountain.

Starting at Cajon Junction on the Barstow Freeway, State Highways 138 and 2, here combined, run westerly, crossing the two transcontinental railroad tracks systems, and gain an area of unusual rock formations known as the Rock Candy Mountains.

Taffy-looking, pocked by wind and weather, suggesting greatly the hiding place for troglodytes, the Rock Candy Mountains, once known as the Mormon Camp Rocks, stand for some distance along the road. Experts claim that they are of much the same formation as the Devil's Punchbowl stones, have simply been offset from that other site by slippage along the San Andreas Fault, a major earthquake rift line that spans the San Gabriel range.

Sideroad into Lone Pine Canyon. Left here is the paved but not scrupulously maintained sideroad into and up Lone Pine Canyon.

Here, in a small valley that parallels the Upper Lytle Creek Ridge and the quarry-pocked Circle Mountain Ridge, is the sleeping place of the San Andreas Fault.

47

The taffy-like Rock Candy Mountains near Cajon Junction.

Strange rock formations in Dev[...]
Punchbowl area near Valyerm[...]

Section of the Rock Candy
Mountain formation near
Cajon Junction.

The road passes the Sharpless Ranch, the Nielson Ranch, the Clyde Ranch—where sweet apples are for sale in season—pokes into pine country near Slover Canyon, climbs above and then drops down into Wrightwood.

Sideroads stand along the byway that lead over into Stockton Flat in the upper Lytle Creek area.

Back on Highways 138-2, the first Joshua trees appear, and here, where the Sales Fire charred the slopes in 1960, is a spectral forest of fire-killed Joshuas. Scrub oak and pinyon pine put in an appearance as we gain Mountain Top Junction, and leave State Highway 138, follow State Highway 2 toward Wrightwood and the Swarthout Valley.

We have left the Joshua trees now, and pinyon puts in a more frequent appearance. The elevation is roughly a mile high here and through a scattering of Jeffrey and ponderosa pine we reach Wrightwood.

Sumner Wright and his brothers came into the region in the early 1900s, built cattle and orchard ranches, and the small community came up around 1924. After the depression of the 1930s the present developers located in the handsome mountain setting and the development of the town as it is known now dates from that point.

Wrightwood is a self-contained small city, in spite of its remote location and resort setting. But the accent here is on recreation. There are riding stables in the area, four motels, nearby ski resorts and winter play areas. Wrightwood has a newspaper and chamber of commerce. Population of the pleasant community is approximately 1,100 permanent residents. Many residents commute to Los Angeles area jobs.

Through Swarthout Valley—named after an early settler—the road heads on toward the northwest. Timber is broken, and high ridges shade the valley.

Here is Holiday Hill, ski resort area, with three chair lifts (the major lift operates each weekend throughout the year, snow or not) and a toboggan area. There are popular long ski runs from the top of Holiday Hill back down to the bottom of the valley.

Big Pines, for many years a popular recreation area, once operated by the Los Angeles County but now a Forest Service facility, is made up of several parts.

The forest station occupies the old Civic Center building.

To the west, on a sideroad, is the Big Pines Recreation Area—divided into Shady Slope Campground and Knob Picnic area—and the Blue Ridge ski resort area, with two chair lifts, ski runs, rentals, etc.

Sideroad, Angeles Crest Highway. The major highway across the top of the Angeles National Forest, which is the extension of State Highway 2, turns west here and runs up over Blue Ridge, past Mt. Baden-Powell into the Waterman, Chilao, Charlton Flat country, back to Red Box, Clear Creek and then down to La Cañada. (See Chapter 3.)

Sideroad to Table Mountain. An additional part of the Big Pines Recreation Area is the Table Mountain complex. The good paved road runs back up the hill to this most modern and most handsome Forest Service campground with trailer sites as well as forty-seven family units. Camping fee here is $1 per night. There are many view points in the campground area where great sweeping panoramas of the desert country to the north are offered. There is a ski resort here, too, with rope tows and Pomo lifts, ski runs, warming huts, rentals.

From this important mountain junction the road to Valyermo drops down now, passes a series of picnic areas and campgrounds on its run down the hill.

50

Forest Service sign welcomes visitor into popular Big Pines area.

Arch Picnic Area stands here, then the Mescal Play Area—a nature trail here by summer—where, by season, a concessionaire rents toboggans and sleds.

The Apple Tree Campground is passed, Peavine Campground, Lake Campground, Mescal Campground, and then small Jackson Lake with Jackson Lake Beach is gained.

Here is the sprawling Mountain Oak Campground in a picturesque setting. As the byway descends the sideroad of Largo Vista Road at Mile High is passed. To the left the green brow of Pinyon Ridge lifts. Joshua trees put in an appearance again as the desert is neared.

There is a glimpse of Valyermo Reservoir off to the right.

Sideroad into Big Rock Creek. At this junction paved Big Rock Creek angles sharply back to the left, the southwest, travels along the stream, shaded with alder and sycamore, past a few cabins, a planting of colorful poplars, to Sycamore Flat Campground, on either side of the road, with twelve family units. The first hint of the Punchbowl country is evident now off to the west: a similar rock formation to the Rock Candy Mountains near Cajon Junction.

The stream widens; there is a turnoff running along an unpaved sideroad to South Fork Campground. A two-mile trail from here leads to the Devil's Punchbowl, a sunken area of strange rock formations including the Devil's Chair.

The Big Rock Creek Road continues, pavement stops, and Big Rock Campground is reached—ten units.

The unpaved road continues on to the Angeles Crest Highway at Vincent Saddle or Gap. (See Chapter 3.)

On north from the Big Rock Creek Junction the Valyermo road passes a cluster of abandoned buildings near the sideroad, right, of the Bob's Gap Road to Victorville.

Then Valyermo, with a district ranger station of the Angeles Na-

*Trees shade Big Rock Creek Road on its sinuous run
south in San Gabriel Mountains high country.*

*Jackson Lake on the road from Big Pines to Valyermo; swimming
is popular here in summer, ice skating can take place in winter.*

tional Forest, is reached. The community is made up largely of orchardists who raise peaches, pears, apples and cherries, and who sell the fruit at roadside stands in season. It was named in 1909 by W. C. Petchner, owner of the Valyermo Ranch. The place name is a combination of two Spanish terms: val, for valley; and yermo, for desert. A post office was operating here as early as 1912.

Beyond the junction community is the sideroad to the left leading back past St. Andrew's Priory, into the Juniper Hills, Cima Mesa country. This is the route the new road into the Devil's Punchbowl takes to the Los Angeles County Park established in 1964.

From this point the road reaches toward Pearblossom and Little Rock.

XII LITTLE ROCK RESERVOIR ROAD

South of Palmdale a brief avenue leads back to a desert-facing reservoir where fishing and boating are popular sports.

Little Rock Reservoir. Cheseboro Road turns south off State Highway 138 roughly three miles west of the community of Little Rock in the southern Antelope Valley and runs due south into Little Rock Creek.

There are jumbo stands of Joshua trees along the way; the road is paved and recently realigned.

Little Rock Reservoir is backed up by a curved concrete dam and provides fishing, boating and swimming in season for users of the Forest Service recreation area.

There is a small resort here, Sahagan's, with supplies as well as boat rentals. The road is unpaved and narrow once it gains the lake, but it travels back past several campgrounds: Juniper Grove, Rocky Point and a Forest Service trailer campground, Joshua Flat.

Beyond the reservoir area the road reaches on back up the creek to the more remote Sycamore Campground, seven miles above the reservoir; and Little Cedars Campground, ten miles above the lake.

From this point the road continues to make junction with the Chilao-Mill Creek Summit truck trail. (See Chapter 3.)

Boating and fishing are popular sports at Little Rock Reservoir.

XIII ANGELES FOREST HIGHWAY

Also known as the Palmdale Cutoff, this range-spanning highway connects the Angeles Crest Highway with the Antelope Valley.

Angeles Forest Highway. In the foothills south of Palmdale, near the junction community of Vincent, is the beginning of the southward running Angeles Forest Highway (a name that often confuses the byway with the Angeles Crest Highway). Designed as a utilitarian avenue rather than a scenic one, the Angeles Forest Highway provides—by using the section of the Angeles Crest Highway from La Cañada to Clear Creek junction—the fastest route from the San Gabriel Valley area to the Antelope Valley. The average driver will find that it takes him a little less than an hour to drive from La Cañada to Vincent, a distance of thirty-three miles.

The first survey for the Angeles Forest Highway was made in 1913. Later, D. J. Macpherson, the engineer who located and built the Mt. Lowe Railway, went over the route and called it feasible. First work on the road was interrupted by World War I. Work started again in the 1930s, and the Angeles Forest Highway —better known to many as the Palmdale cutoff—was finally opened on September 12, 1938.

From Vincent the Angeles Forest Highway gains altitude gradually as it works its way south past the Kentucky Springs country. (Kentucky Springs itself is off the road to the west, difficult to find.)

Sideroad into Santiago Canyon. The unpaved road to the left here leads back over a saddle and steeply down into Santiago Canyon. This is the area where rangers will usually send you if you come to them with a request for a site to target shoot your rifle or shotgun. There are no improved camping or picnicking sites down in the canyon, but it is a large, stream-spraddling area, most handsome by spring.

Sideroad into Aliso Canyon. Paved and opened to the public in 1957, this foothill road bends off to the right, runs down through chaparral past several ranches back toward Acton. Here is the Blum Ranch where apples, honey and nuts are sold.

Into upper Aliso Canyon the Forest Highway climbs, finally gains Mill Creek Summit, 4,900 feet, provides views to the north out toward the desert, and to the south along the Mill Creek drainage.

There is a Forest Service ranger station and residence, and picnic area here.

Sideroad to Mt. Pacifico. To the left here a dirt road passes through the ranger station property and switchbacks up Round Top and then crosses out along the south slope of Pacifico Mountain. (For detailed description of this byway check the sideroad out of Chilao in Chapter 3.)

Sideroad to Mt. Gleason. To the right from Mill Creek Summit an excellent paved road runs up to the Nike base at Mt. Gleason. It is a controlled road; permission must be secured before driving it. The military is usually quite generous with the road, particularly in hunting season. The road now ends for the public at the Nike site: the base is built right across the thoroughfare. Plans are being studied for a flanking road that will bypass the Nike base and will open to the public the attractive high country camps of Messenger Flats and the upper Pacoima regions.

Mt. Gleason, with its impressive timber, has long been eyed as a tourist site. In 1904 in *Over the Range,* Stanley Wood and C. E. Hooper wrote: "Acton is the gateway to the new resort on Mt. Gleason, destined to be one of the great popular pleasure places on the coast." The resort was never built.

From the Mill Creek Summit the Angeles Forest Highway descends into the Mill Creek canyon, runs past a private sideroad leading back to some historic gold mines in the area: the Monte Cristo, the Black Crow, the Black Cargo and the Gold Bar properties.

In this region, scene of a minor gold rush in the 1880s, is supposed to be located the fabled Lost Padres Mine, supplier of gold dust for the mission padres at San Fernando. If the bonanza is here, it has not yet been found.

Here, along the highway and handsomely decorated by streambed trees by spring and fall, is the Mill Creek Picnic Area.

Sideroad to Colby Ranch, Upper Big Tujunga Country. A good dirt road turns left here, climbs the east wall of Mill Creek, descends into a gentle section of the middle Big Tujunga, crosses the stream and runs back to the site of the historic Colby Ranch in Coldwater Canyon. This mountain hideaway and way-station was established by Delos and his wife Lillian in 1891; Colby's wife and daughter were moved to the place in 1896, made the place their home. In time Colby's Ranch, with its orchards and its handsome setting under the great granite cliffs of Strawberry Peak, became a favorite stopping spot with hikers. A gas balloon load of excursionists that was blown from Pasadena in 1909 into the deep snow of the mountainous back country came to rest on Strawberry Peak. The survivors made their way toward Colby's, were rescued and fed there, finally walked out safely.

Colby's is now an organizational camp belonging to the Methodist Church.

59

This handsome bridge spans the Narrows of the Big Tujunga along the Angeles Forest Highway. From this point Forest Highway runs north into historic gold country of Mill Creek.

Beyond Colby's entrance this unpaved byway follows the Upper Big Tujunga, past Wickiup Trail Camp, Wickiup Canyon, scene of gold prospecting in the 1889 rush, on past other side canyons to a return to the Angeles Crest Highway near Shortcut Picnic Area. The road is closed in fire season.

Following the Angeles Forest Highway along the Mill Creek drainage, the private holdings of Angeles Forest Mountain Club, Hidden Springs, Singing Springs are reached. Refreshments and supplies can be purchased at Hidden Springs and Singing Springs.

Through a tunnel the road passes and then comes to the great gorge of the Big Tujunga, spanned by an airy and spectacular bridge. There is turnout space for parking on either side of the bridge, and a view area on the bridge itself for looking down into one of the deepest clefts in this area of the mountains.

From here on to its junction with the Angeles Crest Highway, the Angeles Forest Highway follows a route chiseled out of the great east face of the Big Tujunga. There are many turnouts along the run where glimpses of the Big Tujunga Dam and reservoir may be had.

Sideroad to the Big Tujunga. A good paved road runs west here, parallel to the Big Tujunga all the way to the Sunland-Tujunga area.

Beyond the Big Tujunga side road the Angeles Forest Highway continues its high path along the east wall of the Big Tujunga canyon, arriving at the Clear Creek area and junction with the Angeles Crest Highway.

XIV SOLEDAD CANYON ROAD

Gold mining history is rich along this north edge of the San Gabriel range; and here are the famed Vasquez Rocks.

Soledad Canyon. The new multilaned Antelope Valley Freeway now runs from Solemint Junction to the east end of Mint Canyon north of Acton. Twenty-eight plus miles long, it will cut the driving time from Solemint to Palmdale at least by ten minutes during peak hours.

Running parallel to much of the freeway's course is Soledad Canyon, historic mainly because of the early railway surveys, the building of the Southern Pacific along the streambed—with the driving of the last spike at Lang on September 5, 1876.

The Soledad Canyon Road starts on the northeast corner at a point 1.4 miles west of Vincent. Here the road bends off to the left, runs close at hand to the Southern Pacific tracks across gently rolling canyon bottom country toward Acton.

Sideroad to Aliso Canyon. (See Chapter 13.)

The place name, Acton, was given the community during the years that saw the building of the railroad from Saugus to Mojave: 1873-1876. But more than being a railroad camp, Acton knew a gold mining boom of sorts. There were mines up Aliso Canyon. The names of some of the other canyons in the area indicate mining activity: Arrastre Canyon, Mill Canyon.

The old New York Mine (Governor Mine) between Acton and Palmdale was active first about 1889 and operated sporadically until the 1920s. The Buena Esperanza Mine, northeast of Acton, was first active in 1896.

Placer mining was widespread in the whole Soledad, Santa Clara drainage following the discovery of gold in the 1830s. According to California Division of Mines reports, placering has taken place since the 1830s in Bouquet, Castaic, Cave, Dry, Haskell, Palomas, Placerita, San Francisquito, Santa Felicia, Sheep and Soledad Canyons, but with little activity since the 1930s.

The Falcon Mine, southeast of Acton, saw its most recent activity in 1939-1942 when several hundred tons of gold-silver ore were removed. The Mt. Gleason Mine was the producer of several thousand dollars in gold in the 1890s.

Copper, too, has been mined in the area. The Conover copper mine, on the side of Parker Mountain, came up in 1927-28, saw more recent activity in 1949.

Sideroad to Colombo Lilac Ranch. Near the railroad station of Ravenna a road leads back to the south into the foothills to the Colombo Lilac Ranch where, in season, eastern lilac grows in riotous profusion. Homesick Easterners come on weekends to look and buy the picked blossoms in such quantities that special police are needed to handle the crowds. Usually April sees this wild floral activity. Some of the lilac plants are almost thirty years old, planted by ranch founder Christopher Colombo Brevidoro.

Past narrow ravines leading down from the hills bearing the colorful names of Bootleggers Canyon, Indian Canyon, the Soledad Canyon Road follows the course of the Santa Clara River—most probably the green country sighted by William Manly after his escape from Death Valley in 1849—and comes to the Soledad Ranger Station, with picnic and camping areas.

Sideroad into Agua Dulce Canyon, Vasquez Rocks. Just past the Soledad ranger station is a paved byway turning off to the right. This is the Agua Dulce Canyon Road, and it leads north past a private lake and resort to an intersection with Davenport Road,

Bandit Tiburcio Vasquez hid out in the caves and crannies of Vasquez Rocks in the Soledad Canyon country near Acton.

jogs right, then straightens. A short distance on to the right, along Escondido Canyon Road, is the entrance to the most famous rock formation in Southern California, Vasquez Rocks.

The weather-sculptured, slanting formation has been seen in hundreds of motion pictures and TV films, and is probably the most scenic outcropping this side of Cajon.

Entrance to the well-kept Toney Ranch, on which the rocks are situated, is 50 cents per car. You are given a brief explanatory brochure when you enter.

The fame of the site, of course, comes from the stories that Tiburcio Vasquez, California badman of the 1854-1874 era, pulled into the caves and cul-de-sacs of the rock area to hide after his raids.

There are many good hiding places in the rocks, and youngsters will have a pleasant time climbing the long sloping walls of stone. The Toneys have installed picnic facilities here.

Still standing from a recent TV series production, is the main fort set of "Bengal Lancers." It adds to the local color.

Ed Toney, operator of the 260-acre ranch—tourism is its main commodity—still digs up Indian arrowheads and grinding stones, proving that the caves and crannies were popular even before Vasquez.

Flanking the Soledad Canyon Road on the south after the Agua Dulce turnoff is the 4,785-foot prominence of Magic Mountain, atop of which sits an abandoned Nike missile site.

At Lang is the historical marker calling attention to the driving of the last spike that united the two sections of the Southern Pacific Railroad. On hand for the ceremonies that September day in 1876 were Governor Leland Stanford, Collis P. Huntington and others.

From Lang the Soledad Canyon Road runs on west—with the new freeway very much in evidence now along an ever-broadening Santa Clara River.

Sideroad to Sand Canyon. Both to the right and left here runs the Sand Canyon Road. To the right it is a short length of byway that curves out to the Mint Canyon road, Sierra Highway, U.S. Highway 6 near Forest Park.

To the left the Sand Canyon Road is the northern extension of the Little Tujunga Road. (See Chapter 23.)

The Soledad Canyon Road, for our purposes, ends at Solemint Junction, where it crosses Sierra Highway, U.S. Highway 6.

XV MINT CANYON ROAD

Once the only way to get from the Los Angeles area to the Antelope Valley, historic Mint Canyon anticipates less traffic with the opening of the new Antelope Valley Freeway.

Mint Canyon. The Mint Canyon road used to be the principal way to get from Saugus to the Antelope Valley. It was a rugged road in those days—or were automobiles that much different? Cars boiled (there is still a site called Boiling Point on some maps) as they struggled over the route. Later the Soledad Canyon Road was improved, and some people preferred that byway. Now with the new Antelope Valley Freeway cutting a great arc from Solemint to Palmdale, Mint Canyon will probably become another ghost avenue as far as tourist traffic is concerned.

Starting at Vincent and working back toward Los Angeles there is little to distinguish the road—Sierra Highway it is signed, U.S. Highway 6.

At Vincent in the old days there was a great railroad Y where trains turned around. That and many of the roadside signs of gold mining are gone today.

To the right of the highway is the wind-buffeted Sierra Pelona Ridge country where 90- and 100-mile-an-hour winds have been recorded at the Forest Service lookout tower.

Here on the left is the sideroad to Acton; here is the sideroad to Agua Dulce and Vasquez Rocks (see Chapter 14). The Sierra Pelona Valley is crossed. Small resorts, roadside honey shops are passed. A run of the freeway here interrupts the old Mint Canyon road.

Here, again on the left, is the Davenport Road turnoff, leading back to the howlite collecting area of Tick Canyon, and on to Agua Dulce and Vasquez Rocks.

The Sand Canyon sideroad is passed, again on the left, and finally Solemint Junction is gained.

Roughly five miles south of Solemint Junction on U.S. Highway 6, is a crossroads.

Sideroad into Placerita Canyon, the Oak of the Golden Dream.
Placerita Canyon Road runs both ways from Highway 6. To the right it leads through to main Saugus-Newhall Road, passing the burned remnants of the old Gene Autry Melody Ranch, scene of much TV filming, including an endless number of "Gunsmoke" sequences.

To the left the byway leads into Placerita Canyon State Park, an oak and sycamore shaded canyon area dedicated to the first discovery of gold in California by Francisco Lopez in 1842. (Actually old records talk about gold in the area as early as 1838.)

The discovery of gold here is a classic story now, oft retold.

Lopez was out riding across the oak-studded rolling hills. It was March 1842, and the hills were green with new grass. At noon he stopped under one of the big oaks for his lunch. With his hunting knife he dug up a clump of wild onions that grew beneath the tree. Clinging to the roots of the onions were bright particles of gold.

The discovery created enormous excitement in the Del Valle's Rancho San Francisco. Samples of gold were sent to Mexico. Indians and Spaniards flocked to the site and started winnowing the golden flakes from the sandy soil. In November of 1842 the first gold from Newhall was shipped from the Newhall placers to the U.S. Mint in Philadelphia. That year the diggings produced almost $10,000.

Today the discovery spot is known as the "Oak of the Golden Dream." To find the actual spot, park your car inside the preserve

68

and walk west along the watercourse, past the entrance road. Climb up the north bank of the stream and here, set under a clump of trees, is the historical marker.

A pageant is usually staged in the park in early summer commemorating the event.

On south now, past the fork where the Saugus-Newhall road rejoins U.S. Highway 6, over the low summit here, past the unmarked site of the historic old Newhall tunnel, we come to a turnout area on the left flanked by several historical markers.

This is the site of the famous—or infamous—old San Fernando Pass, or, as it is called, old Fremont Pass, at one time, before the tunnel and the cut, the route north.

Hundreds of words were written in the old days about the difficulty of the old San Fernando Pass. Right at the summit there was a four-foot step up, or down, depending on your direction, that usually saw stage riders getting out and pushing.

Don Gaspar de Portola traveled the historic crossing on August 8, 1769. In January 1847, John C. Fremont gave his name to the pass when he traversed the Newhall area on his way from Santa Barbara to Los Angeles. In 1859 General E. F. Beale and his men removed fifty feet of earth from the gap so that stages could make the crossing with less difficulty. But even then the toll road was so steep that the tollmaster kept horses ready to assist wagons over the incline. At the top wagons, and even early automobiles, had their wheels chained for the descent.

It is an easy scramble down into a wash and then up into the defile for a look at Beale's Cut. It is a rare piece of pioneer road building, perhaps the oldest in California.

Highway 6 ceases to be of interest to us beyond its junction with U.S. Highway 99.

Historic Beale's Cut, which changed Fremont Pass from a night-mare into a passable wagon road. Cut was made in 1859.

XVI BOUQUET CANYON ROAD

A deep canyon region of pleasant summer homes and camp sites north of Saugus is explored by this fine mountain road.

Bouquet Canyon. (In order to provide a kind of order to help the guidebook user explore this corner of the San Gabriel Mountains, the trip through the following canyons is taken first up canyon, then down: Bouquet Canyon, down; San Francisquito Canyon, up; Elizabeth Lake Canyon, down; Old Ridge Route, up.)

Old records label this canyon through the northwest corner of the San Gabriel Mountains Deadman's Canyon, and El Potrero de Chico Lopez, the latter after the early owner of the property along its lower reaches.

One of Lopez's vaqueros, a settler in the area, Francisco Chari, was a former sailor and his many stories about "el buque," the ship, earned him and the canyon the title "buque," a word which has been conveniently corrupted by a procession of geographers into "bouquet."

The canyon knew traffic in the old days in spite of a difficult passage near The Falls. It has known floods, gold prospecting, grizzly bears and from its mouth on the north, in the old days, great herds of antelope could be seen out on the plain. Some claim antelope can still be found in certain badland regions of the upper Antelope Valley and the Tehachapi Mountains.

Starting on the Leona Valley Road—and the San Andreas Fault —the Bouquet Canyon road runs west through typical desert-side dwarf chaparral, gains Lincoln Crest, 3,619 feet, travels in the shadow of the Sierra Pelona Ridge past Twin Oaks and Two Shay

Ranch. The intersection with the Spunky Canyon Road is gained at the Bouquet Canyon Reservoir.

Sideroad to Spunky Canyon, Green Valley, San Francisquito Canyon. A good paved byway, built around 1925, leads right here, up over Spunky Canyon Saddle, down past picturesque Spunky Canyon Campground, seven units, into pleasant Green Valley— it earned this name because of the green tint of the area due to the many live oaks.

Dowd Canyon was an earlier place name here, according to old-timers who recall a homesteader of the 1890s by that name. Grizzly bears were common in the region here.

Today Green Valley is one of the most attractive settlements in the northwest corner of the range. Snow calls by winter and by summer cool breezes manage to slip through the oaked canyon. There are between 400-500 permanent residents, now several stores.

The sideroad finally runs into the San Francisquito Canyon Road. (See Chapter 17.)

Bouquet Reservoir, part of the City of Los Angeles Water and Power complex, was built in 1929 and can hold 36,500 acre feet of water, floods part of the old Biddison, Sears, Nimmo and Malone homesteads settled in the 1890s.

As this is drinking water storage, there are no recreational facilities on the reservoir, which, in recent drought years, has been low.

Sideroad to Sierra Pelona Lookout, Big Oak Trail. A marked unpaved sideroad to the left here leads back to frequently wind-buffeted Sierra Pelona lookout. An interesting hike can be reached via this sideroad. Drive five miles from the Bouquet Canyon Road to Sierra Pelona Ridge, turn left, drive 0.7 miles to the beginning

72

of the California Riding and Hiking trail going down the hill. It is 3.2 miles down the trail to the Bouquet Canyon Road. About halfway down is the record canyon live oak on the Angeles National Forest. It measures 37 feet 4 inches in circumference (at ground level on the high side). The tree lies about ⅛ mile west of the main trail, about a five minute walk.

Near the top of Sierra Pelona Ridge the visitor will see a large outcropping of stone known locally as "ribbon rock." The name comes from unusual stratification. It is preserved by the National Forest for studies by the public as well as geologists.

There is little point in following the Sierra Pelona dirt road beyond these points.

Past Bouquet Reservoir the Bouquet Canyon Road starts to descend now, past The Falls Campground, store and restaurant, and a fine place for younsgters who like rock scrambles; a waterfall about 25 feet high stands here.

The canyon bottom road was built around 1904, partly by the settlers of the upper canyon area who wanted more direct access route to Saugus-Newhall area. Most tricky portion of the building came in The Falls area.

There are a procession of smaller Forest Service campgrounds then as Bouquet Canyon Road works its sinuous way south. Cabins and summer homes stand here, many decorated with the unique Bouquet Canyon stone. Permission to gather small portions of the colored flagstone can be obtained from the district ranger station at Newhall (there is a small fee). For those who desire larger quantities of the building rock there are commercial quarries in the canyon.

Big Oaks Lodge and a forest station are passed. Here the canyon puts on its most handsome guise: shaded and deep with a running stream. Here is the Bouquet Canyon store, then the Forest Service's Texas Canyon station and headquarters for its area hotshot crew of crack fire fighters. There is a sideroad here back into the Texas Canyon country.

An area of unusual rock formation, known since the old days as The Pinnacles, is passed. Here stands Coarse Gold Canyon, hinting of earlier mining days. Here is a sideroad into Vasquez Canyon.

Then turkey ranches, abandoned farms, dilapidated farm houses mixed with the more modern. Some cattle spreads, streamside cottonwoods as the canyon widens and runs past the San Francisquito Canyon Road and gains Bouquet Junction.

74

XVII   SAN FRANCISQUITO CANYON ROAD

One of the earliest-known routes through the barrier mountains, San Francisquito Canyon Road knew the terrible St. Francis Dam disaster in 1928.

San Francisquito Canyon. Starting at the south end of the road, at the junction with the Bouquet Canyon Road, San Francisquito Canyon Road runs north past subdivision, school, scattered farms into less civilized country.

To get a clear perspective of this canyon, it is necessary to go back in history. San Francisquito Canyon is the first route through the northwest corner of the San Gabriel Mountains. It was an established road in 1854 when Robert Stockton Williamson conducted his railroad survey. That it had been here for many years prior to that date is substantiated by reports of settlers, mountain men, explorers who used it as the only avenue north from Los Angeles to the San Joaquin Valley.

Up until the opening of the Ridge Route in 1914 it would maintain the role of the main avenue through this up and down country.

But the most memorable day in history for San Francisquito Canyon was later than that. March 12, 1928, is the date. Shortly after midnight that night the 185-foot high, two-year-old St. Francis dam, impounding water from Owens Valley for the people of Los Angeles, went out.

The wall of water that rushed down the canyon destroyed everything in its path on a 65-mile race to the sea. Hundreds of houses were destroyed, not only in the canyon itself but along the Santa Clara watercourse in places like Piru, Fillmore and Santa Paula.

The loss of life, a figure never really firmed because of unrecovered bodies and transients that were killed, approached 500. Orchards, farms, cattle ranches, apiaries were ruined, buried under mud.

The 1225-foot wide dam, ruptured by the disaster so that either side washed away leaving a column of masonry in the center of the canyon-spanning arc, was never rebuilt.

This background is helpful in any exploration of the canyon. All that country south of the wreckage of the St. Francis Dam, was scoured clean in 1928.

Proceeding up canyon, past stands of sycamore and cottonwood that decorate the slight stream that stands here, the first of two powerhouses is reached. This is Powerhouse No. 2, and from over the ridge behind it snake three great pipes carrying water to turn the generators.

This water, in this leg of its trip from the Owens Valley country, starts at Fairmont Reservoir on the southern edge of the Antelope Valley, follows a tube burrowed through the flinty mountains to Powerhouse No. 1, then by tunnel and pipes reaches Powerhouse No. 2, and thence, via tube and pipes to Dry Canyon Reservoir to the east.

Between Powerhouse No. 2 and the Los Angeles County Detention Camp 17, on the west side of the road, is what is left of that last pillar of the old St. Francis Dam. Dun in color, with some reinforcing metal sticking out of it, it dominates a small flat. There is an unpaved turnoff here, evidence that many cars have stopped and their passengers have looked and remembered.

In the area of the detention camp the work on a new San Francisquito Canyon road is apparent. This is an inmate project, may be finished all the way to Green Valley by 1966. Sections of the highway in various stages of completion are in evidence.

There is a small settlement at Powerhouse No. 1. This station is open to the public and is interesting to visit.

*Public is invited to visit interior of Powerhouse No. 1
in San Francisquito Canyon.*

Beyond Powerhouse No. 1 pavement ends. The byway will stay unpaved for five miles, all the way to Green Valley. At first the road is narrow, steep, winding and follows the edge of a steep drop-off. Yet with care flatland drivers can drive the spookier section. The road quickly levels, straightens and flattens out as the upper canyon is reached.

Sideroad into South Portal Canyon. A marked unpaved sideroad turns off to the left here, leads back into South Portal Canyon, South Portal Campground, and to an interesting access tunnel to the Fairmont-to-San Francisquito Canyon underground aqueduct.

South Portal Campground, about a mile in from the San Francisquito Canyon road, is shaded by giant live oaks, is situated on a number of benches and flats along the stream—a most handsome setting.

Beyond the campground a white concrete shell stands beside the canyon-bottom road. This is an old transformer building. To the west here, at the foot of the hill, is the gated access tunnel that leads 1,300 feet back to the main water tunnel. This shaft is used when work on the larger tunnel is required.

The area around this South Portal tunnel was once a boom camp, a city of 500 souls during the years between 1905-1906 and 1912 while the big tunnel was being bored out of the mountain. South Portal, it was called, and evidence that a town once stood here can be found on the chaparraled flats along the canyon walls.

This road—strictly a Forest Service truck trail—continues back to Spruce Spring, the Tule Canyon Truck Trail, Grassy Mountain, Munz Lake and back to San Francisquito Canyon north of Green Valley.

Back on the San Francisquito Canyon road the edge of live oak colored Green Valley—hence its name—is gained. When pavement begins again there is a fork.

Handsome oak-shaded South Portal Campground in San Franciscquito Canyon country.

Sideroad through Green Valley to Bouquet Canyon. Running east, this good paved road passes through the heart of Green Valley, the several small stores and the many attractive homes, past the Spunky Canyon Campground, seven units, over Spunky Saddle into Bouquet Canyon.

From the resumption of pavement San Francisquito Canyon Road runs on north, past San Francisquito Campground, ten units, and Forest Station, toward a low summit.

Sideroad to Grassy Mountain. The signed, unpaved truck trail to Grassy Mountain might frighten the most confirmed freeway driving flatlander, but the reward is the spectacular view from the bald summit. It is possible not only to see the whole Green Valley, upper San Francisquito panorama, but distant Sierra Pelona Ridge, and to the north the wrinkled floor of the Antelope Valley. The road up is narrow, a little steep, but solid and well footed. And there is almost no traffic.

Past the Grassy Mountain turnoff San Francisquito Road continues down grade to its end at the Leona Valley road.

XVIII

ELIZABETH LAKE
CANYON ROAD

The road signs call this canyon-following byway the Lake Hughes Road now; its campgrounds are famous.

Elizabeth Lake Canyon, Lake Hughes Road. According to old-timers a wagon track stood up this canyon around 1875. Anything before might have been a horse trail, for it is known that prospectors combed the area in that first sweep of gold interest around the 1830s and 1840s. But most of the gold action came about fifty years later.

Names on the land here, as elsewhere, are interesting and descriptive and conjure up pictures of the land. For instance, there is Ruby Canyon and Red Mountain; Necktie Canyon and Necktie Basin (a grim suggestion); Red Fox Canyon, Turkey Canyon, Deer Canyon; all tributary to Elizabeth Lake. The name of the main canyon stood as early as 1853, but historians have not nailed down the identity of the Elizabeth after whom the lake and canyon drew their name.

From the settlement of Lake Hughes on the Elizabeth Lake-Pine Canyon Road the canyon byway runs southwest, is signed the Lake Hughes Road, sees the walls of the ravine pinch in, with sycamore, alder, cottonwood and willow standing along the creek bottom.

Cottonwood Campground, one of the district's recently rehabilitated sites, twenty units, is located at a spot where stream and canyon widen. Great patriarchal cottonwoods grow here, shading another one of the show campgrounds in the Forest. Water comes from old-fashioned hand pumps, a picturesque sight found in several area Forest Service camps.

At Cottonwood is one of the Forest Service's interesting self-conducting nature tours. There are twenty-odd stops along this half-mile trail, and the gratis mimeographed brochure is keyed to describe various chaparral plants, native trees, geological formations, points of interest in the campground. This self-conducted nature walk idea, first installed on the Forest in 1962, puts more meaning into a random outing, has proved popular with children and adults.

On to the southwest now the canyon snakes, with the walls lifting steeply on both sides. Here is Elizabeth Lake Canyon Campground, a smaller site, with eight family units.

The byway passes the Warm Springs Rehabilitation Camp, operated by the Department of Charities, County of Los Angeles.

Sideroad to Warm Springs Canyon, East Fork of Fish Canyon, Cienega Campground.

An unpaved Forest Service road runs to the right here, back bordering Warm Springs Canyon, over the saddle into the Rattlesnake Canyon and East Fork of Fish Canyon country. Here is the Cienega Campground, oak shaded, with water, and a great favorite with Boy Scouts.

To the right of the Cienega Campground a rough dirt road reaches up Fish Canyon and deadends at the Pianobox Prospect. From here it is an easy hike back into the Fish Canyon Narrows, a slot in the mountains sometimes only a few yards wide, with steep canyon walls. The trail fords the stream many times, and typical streamside trees are present. This is a most delightful hike, with almost no climb involved, for almost a half mile, as the slot wriggles deeper into the back country. To the north of the narrow canyon the country opens up and there can be found evidences of old mining operations. The trail goes on all the way to the Sawmill country.

Continuing past Cienega Campground to the west we make the

passage down Fish Canyon where the rocky canyon walls press in and stream bed and road are one. Here the road is a heavy duty concrete causeway, hopefully floodproof. The road runs into Castaic Canyon which joins Elizabeth Lake Canyon near its southern end.

Sideroad from Warm Springs along Ruby Canyon. To the east from Warm Springs another unpaved Forest Service road runs along Ruby Canyon, finally gains San Francisquito Canyon at Powerhouse No. 1.

From Warm Springs the Elizabeth Lake Canyon byway continues southwest, passing the Elizabeth Lake Forest Station, cabins, organizational camp, and Taylor Campground—ten units.

Now the canyon widens as we enter Castaic Valley, the sideroad into Cienega Canyon is passed.

Here, still some years in the future, a great barrier, the Castaic Dam, may stand one day. A part of the Feather River Water Project, the Castaic Dam would hold back 350,000 acre feet of water, would provide a recreational lake, would flood Castaic Canyon and Elizabeth Lake Canyon back almost to the forest station.

The scars on the sidehills here are where engineers are conducting test drillings for proper dam footings.

We now pass the sideroad on the right that is the Old Ridge Route and come to Castaic where the road ends.

XIX OLD RIDGE ROUTE

The Old Ridge Route of 1914-1933 still stands and driving the narrow, twisting, ridge-following road is like stepping back in time 50 years.

The Old Ridge Route. From Castaic the Old Ridge Route is gained by driving east along the road up Elizabeth Lake Canyon (the road sign reads Lake Hughes Road) about one mile, then turning left on the paved sideroad there.

This is maintained portion of the historic old road, and here the road is always wide enough for passing. Beyond in spots slides and undercuttings have chewed the road down to one lane. But the old highway is never dangerous, really never very spooky although in its day, with heavy traffic, it was a man-killer.

There are a few ranch houses up this preliminary leg of the Old Ridge, and then you come to a gate pronouncing "End of maintained public road." Do not be dismayed. The road beyond the sign is safe for cautious drivers and will take you back in time close to fifty years.

The Old Ridge Route, which actually follows the crest of a ridge or close to it during much of its meanderings, began in 1914 and took the place of the older, slower road up San Francisquito Canyon. For cars of the day it was a terror: steep, winding, narrow. During its reign it overcame some of its disadvantages. Its original concrete ribbon was widened by macadam, curves were gentled and straightened, more turnouts were built.

The original 48.36 miles of Old Ridge Route from Castaic to the Grapevine had 39,441 degrees of curve, roughly 110 complete circles.

*Looking south toward Castaic with the Old Ridge Route
on the left, the new Ridge Route on the right.*

The newer Ridge Route opened in 1933, a magnificent, wide avenue. The Old Ridge Route ghosted overnight and the long parade of gas stations, tourist cabins, resorts, lunch counters were bypassed.

Almost every trace of these is gone now. You'll still find foundations and clearings at places like Old Reservoir Summit and Tumble Inn. Sandberg's stood for years, burned recently.

While the drive is never high speed, it is nostalgic. In several places the old wooden guard rail still stands. The side canyons have been combed by antique car collectors who have picked up the wrecks of old cars for their now-valuable spare parts.

There are numerous side roads, some leading down to the left, back to U.S. Highway 99. Others lead down to the right into Castaic Canyon.

Roughly twenty-five miles north of Castaic is the only major sideroad:

Sideroad to Liebre Mountain, the Sawmill-Liebre Country. It is three miles up a steep, narrow, switchbacked Forest Service truck trail to Liebre Mountain, 5,085 feet, atop of which perches the Forest Service's old shingled West Liebre lookout tower.

There is a small campground near here, and the road, flat and easy to drive, follows east out along the backbone of mountain. It is a pleasant drive during most of the year. The unpaved byway passes through handsome stands of black and scrub oak, and as it nears Sawmill Campground, a hunters' camp, pines put in a showing.

The sideroad forks, and the driver can drop down to the Pine Canyon Road. A narrow, steep branch sideroad along the way leads to Atmore Meadows—dead end—and a hunters' camp. Upper Shake Campground can be reached from this byway.

Back on the Old Ridge Route, the ribbon of old concrete con-

Old shingled lookout tower atop Liebre peak overlooking Ridge Route Country.

tinues northward, returns to maintained status near fire-gutted Sandberg's.

At the junction of Quail Lake Fire Station sideroads lead west one and a half miles of easy road to the U.S. Weather Station atop Bald Mountain (visitors welcome); north to State Highway 138; east via the West Oakdale Canyon Road to Three Points and Pine Canyon Road.

The Old Ridge Route is rewarding to drive for many reasons. It is one of the best preserved examples of a yesterday highway. By keeping an eye solely on the ribbon of concrete the implication of the endless curves becomes apparent. The Old Ridge Route is pleasant to drive because it is seldom busy. Few casual tourists tackle it beyond the "not maintained" signs. Yet, except during bad weather, it is as safe as many more tended mountain roads. Best reason of all to drive the historic byway: imagine the old-time cars back on the grade, their struggles with boiling radiators from one free water station to the next. Put the big old trucks back on the route—and feel a little sorry for the pioneer motorists who had to drive the route.

XX LEONA VALLEY, ELIZABETH LAKE, PINE CANYON ROADS

Following atop the San Andreas Fault this highway runs from Palmdale to the new Ridge Route, offering many scenic sideroads.

Leona Valley Road, Elizabeth Lake Road, Pine Canyon Road.
From Palmdale a fine paved avenue, signed at the beginning Palmdale Boulevard, runs west along the San Andreas Fault toward the Leona Valley.

In the beginning, before the canyon country is reached, this is typical modern desert real estate, with subdivisions, new communities like Desert View Highlands.

The byway changes its name; it becomes Avenue O, meets the first of the Joshua trees, finds patches of juniper as the wide canyon begins to pinch in.

Leona Valley, which is entered via Amargosa Creek, draws its name from Miguel Leonis, pioneer settler in the area. Cottonwood trees mark spots where streams run in season; but mainly this is desert country, with typical cover of sage, buckwheat, yucca and Joshua trees growing on the usually browned slopes. Only the heavy rainfall of an exceptional winter, followed by the smiling warmth of spring, brings greenness to these hills.

There are hunting clubs in the area, and one of these is passed, the Ritter Ranch, at the sideroad to Quartz Hill. The road bears its correct title now: Elizabeth Lake Road, and it continues generally westward through the gentle Leona Valley.

Sideroad into Bouquet Canyon. At the local landmark of the Leona School is the paved sideroad down into Bouquet Canyon,

89

a pleasant mountain canyon drive with many attractive campgrounds. The road debouches at Bouquet Junction just north of Saugus. (See Chapter 16.)

Farms are passed now; the little community of Leona Valley, with its post office and stores, is gained. From here it is possible to drive south and west into the cluster of rural homes that is Lost Valley.

Sideroad to San Francisquito Canyon. Roughly six and a half miles beyond the Bouquet Canyon sideroad is another, this one into Green Valley and then on down San Francisquito Canyon, past the two powerhouses, and finally joining Bouquet Canyon Road just north of Bouquet Junction. (See Chapter 17.)

An old adobe stands along the road here, its early history clouded in the many stories of the region. Here is a concrete tower, not a silo, as it looks, but once a power substation. Sideroads to the right reach out toward Del Sur and the Antelope Valley on the far side of Portal Ridge.

Then the tree-ringed, marshy area that is the sometimes Elizabeth Lake is passed; the modern, well-kept resort of Munz Lake is passed; pines begin to put in an appearance along the road.

Within the boundaries once again of the Angeles National Forest, this is the Lake Hughes Mountain Resort area. The community of Lake Hughes is reached: stores, restaurants, post office.

Sideroad into Elizabeth Lake Canyon. The sideroad to the left here leads down Elizabeth Lake Canyon and is signed the Lake Hughes Road, a bit confusing. Down this byway lies the pleasant Cottonwood Campground, about four miles, and the road runs on through to Castaic at its end. (See Chapter 18.)

Past Lake Hughes the pines are less shy, the road begins to climb and it bears a different name now: the Pine Canyon Road.

90

But both its direction and its destination remain unchanged.

Just short of the Pine Canyon Forest Station is a small parking area, fine for picnicking in the car.

Just beyond the forest station is the sideroad to the left leading back to Lower Shake Campground, seven family units. Then the sideroad to the left that will lead up the high ridge above and run through the Sawmill-Liebre country all the way to the Old Ridge Route. (See Chapter 22.)

Timberline Meadow Resort offers fee camping in a pleasant setting in the pines and oaks. The sideroad to the right leads back to private Lake Tweedy.

Three Points. Pine Canyon Road bends sharply to the left here and the sideroad, Three Points Road, runs north to a junction with State Highway 138.

Black oak, some buckeye, pine make a showing now as the road climbs. Horse Trail Campground, seven units, is here.

On some maps this stretch of highway is called the West Oak-dale Canyon Road, and it follows Oakdale Canyon generally at the beginning, then gets more serious about climbing to the Quail Lake Fire Station.

Junction. To the east here, along the way we have come, is the Pine Canyon or West Oakdale Canyon Road. To the north a lateral running out to State Highway 138. To the west a byway climbs Bald Mountain to the U.S. Weather Station there—open to the public. To the south is the Old Ridge Route, an interesting drive down to Castaic via the 1914-1919 built Ridge Route.

XXI LITTLE TUJUNGA

North of Sylmar and San Fernando is this road that climbs into the Pacoima country, then seeks out the Soledad Canyon on the north.

Little Tujunga. The Tujunga drainages are among the main tributaries of the famous Los Angeles River. The Little Tujunga, or Little T, lies directly behind the Hansen Flood Control Basin above San Fernando. From Foothill the Little T road can be reached by Osborne Street. Past the side canyon of Kagel, the Little T Forest Station is gained.

The Little Tujunga is wide here, boulder-strewn, scarred by floods.

As we continue north we pass a scattering of ranches, come to a sideroad back into Gold Creek canyon, a pleasant oak-shaded ravine that ends at the entrance of the old C. B. DeMille Paradise Ranch, where many motion pictures were filmed in the old days. An organizational camp also lies back in this Gold Creek tributary.

Here is a small picnic area, and the road climbs now, gains Dillon Divide, passing turnouts that offer fine views of the lower canyon, a hideaway ranch perched on a remote flat below.

Sideroad into Pacoima country. At Dillon Divide a sideroad leads off to the right back into the Pacoima Creek drainage. Here are two small Forest Service campgrounds: Honeybee with four family units and Dutch Louie with six. The good, though typically narrow, sometimes steep, sometimes rough Forest Service road, reaches back all the way to the Mt. Gleason country, but deadends there because of the Nike base. A loop can be made in this no-pavement back country, however, to the north where the Pacoima Road connects with the Messenger Flats-Magic Mountain road. Via this latter back country road a return can be made to the Little T highway. Most of the back country road junctions are posted. Or, pick up an area map from the nearest forest station before making your trip.

Past Dillon Divide the Little T road continues north past the old Dillon Ranch, losing altitude now. Here is the Rainbow Wood trout farm, a private campground with trout fishing and picnicking facilities. Fir mingles with cottonwood and sycamores along the canyon walls and bottom.

At Bear Divide there are sideroads off to each side: to the left is the paved avenue up to the active Nike complex on Los Pinetos; to the right the paved road back to the abandoned Nike installation on Magic Mountain, which connects with the Pacoima drainage byway.

From Bear Divide north the Little T road is called the Bear Canyon Road. It continues to descend, reaches the springtime-pretty campground of Live Oak, in the mouth of Bear Canyon, with twelve family units.

Then the wider country of Sand Canyon is reached, homes and farms stand along the pleasant fields. We pass on the left the sideroad in Placerita Canyon, its state park and the site where Francisco Lopez first found gold in California.

The road runs on out to the Santa Clara River, the Soledad Canyon road and the new Antelope Valley Freeway near Solemint Junction.

XXII BIG TUJUNGA

Another historic area is opened by this byway north out of Sunland-Tujunga, following a watercourse that has known disastrous flooding.

Big Tujunga. Like other sites in the San Gabriel Mountains, gold is woven into the fabric of this canyon. At the lower end of the canyon is tributary Gold Canyon, suggesting early-day placering. At the upper end, along Wickiup Creek and especially Mill Creek, there was considerable gold hunting activity.

A work road up the canyon has existed for years. Pedro Ybarra was one of the first to settle in the canyon. The Ybarra Ranch, still a landmark in the Big Tujunga, was founded in 1880 when the elder Ybarra planted an orchard, a vineyard, and built a cabin and corral in the lower reaches of the canyon.

In 1900 Lon Chapin, artist for a Los Angeles newspaper, found the canyon, liked what he saw, and built a cabin in the middle reaches. Dr. Homer Hansen, who had first come to the Big Tujunga in the 1880s, returned and built a two-story lodge. The structure was destroyed by flood in 1926, was rebuilt, but the greater flood of 1938 erased all but the sentinel stone fireplaces of Hansen's Lodge.

In 1915 the first survey was made for a flood control project in the canyon. It wasn't until 1931 that the Big Tujunga dam was completed and in the 1938 flood it was badly silted. Constant sluicing away of silt today makes the deep pools along the Big Tujunga unsuitable for trout planting.

It was in February 1938 that the placid canyon stream became a raging millrace. Water five feet high boiled over the spillway at

94

Ruins of old mountain resort frame new bridge across Big Tujunga near Angeles Forest Highway.

the flood control dam. The dam's flood gates were also thrown open. A wall of brown water fifteen feet high foamed down through the canyon, sweeping up cabins, roads, trees, everything in its path. The floodwaters spilled out across the San Fernando Valley and into the Los Angeles River. One life was lost during the disaster.

As soon as debris from the 1938 flood was cleared away, engineers were planning a new road up the canyon. An extension of Mt. Gleason Avenue in Sunland-Tujunga, the road follows the wide canyon bottom back. At first a canyon bottom road was built, but this is bypassed now by a high road, started in 1952. The first bridge here was completed in 1953 taking the road to Vogel Flat, and the settlement along Paloma Flat.

Down canyon from Vogel Flat, at Trail Canyon on the left, is a scattering of cabins, and four trailside camps on a hike—no road —toward Mt. Gleason.

At Vogel Flat there is a forest station and a picnic area with fourteen family units.

Via the high road the byway continues back to the impressive concrete arch bridge, opened in September 1958, which spans the Big Tujunga just downstream from the ruins of the old Hanson Lodge.

The scars from fires can be seen back in this country. The first recorded blaze to char the Big Tujunga was in 1878. U.S. Forest Service documents show that a fire then burned from Glendale's foothills all the way across the San Gabriel Mountains to a point overlooking the desert. There have been other fires in 1896, in 1900, 1919, 1925, 1947 and 1959.

Upstream from the high bridge—the chasm here is 274 feet wide, 130 feet deep—is the great Big Tujunga Dam. From viewpoints further on, and along the Angeles Forest Highway, good views of dam and reservoir can be had.

There is an area under the bridge and then upstream that cries for recreational development; the setting is streamside and woodsy.

From the bridge the road angles sharply upward, gaining at last the Angeles Forest Highway. The byway is used by sight-seers largely, but is also heavily employed by Sunland-Tujunga area residents on their way to and from the Antelope Valley area. For this purpose the Big Tujunga—Big T—road is a timesaver.

XXIII MT. LOWE

The famous Mt. Lowe Railroad was built in 1893, ran until 1938. Some of the ruins of the fantastic sky conquering rail line still exist.

Mt. Lowe. The Mt. Lowe Railway is gone now—the victim of fire, flood and unbelievable apathy. The old roadbeds have eroded until they barely support footpaths. The ravine-spanning culverts and bridges have vanished. Almost all traces of buildings atop the mountains have been erased.

Yet here stood an incredible monument to man's engineering ability. For almost half a century the ride up to Mt. Lowe was talked about all over the nation by tourists who had come and ridden the awesome thing, and then gone home to tell a tale of wonder.

That the ride had charm, there is no doubt. Whether or not its death was untimely is no question to put to a sentimentalist.

The idea of a railroad up the slope of Pasadena-facing front country of the San Gabriel range was talked about as early as 1886. Mt. Wilson then was the upper destination. That year it was proposed to build "a good bridle-road first, and then enlist eastern capitalists to build a hotel up there, and build a cog-wheel railroad from the mouth of Eaton Canyon up to it." The cog-wheel railroad idea faded as the Mt. Wilson Toll Road came into being.

After that only talk persisted about a mountain railroad; the action was lacking.

It was engineer D. J. Macpherson in January 1890 who went to the mountains with a few assistants and made the first bona fide survey that the mountains knew.

He first searched out Las Flores and Rubio Canyon. He investigated Eaton Canyon and still sought out Wilson's Peak.

Professor Thaddeus S. C. Lowe, inventor and Civil War balloonist, became interested in the idea, looked over the mountains, rejected a terminus at Mt. Wilson largely because speculators had already staked out the claims on Mt. Wilson's summit and, with Macpherson, charted a new route.

The railroad would run up Rubio Canyon to a station there. Thence by incline passengers would be taken to the top of Echo Mountain where a small settlement would grow. From Echo Mountain, via a winding, cliff-hanging route, an electric car would run on back to Crystal Springs where the Alpine Tavern, end-of-the-line hotel would be built.

The first regular passenger cars up to the Rubio Pavilion ran on June 29, 1893. The Great Incline, a 3,000-foot climb by stair-stepped cars traveling up a 60 per cent average grade and rising from 2,200-feet elevation at Rubio to 3,500 at Echo, opened to the public on July 4, 1893.

Atop Echo Mountain were two hotels: The Chalet, and the Echo Mountain House; plus a giant searchlight, an observatory and other buildings. It was called The White City.

From Echo Mountain a narrow gauge trolley wound back around 127 curves and over eighteen trestles to the Alpine Tavern. Where there were spectacular curves or points of interest, they were given names: Cape of Good Hope, Horseshoe Curve, Circular Bridge, Dawn Station, Sunset Point, Granite Gate, Grand Canyon and finally Ye Alpine Tavern.

At the top there were many hikes offered, the one out to Inspiration Point being the most popular.

You could hike or take the famous Pony Train up to the summit of Mt. Lowe if you wished; management furnished riding skirts for the ladies and "koveralls" for men for 25 cents each.

99

In a series of storms and fires The White City was destroyed. On September 15, 1936, the Alpine Tavern and most of the buildings around it burned. There were tentative plans to rebuild but not quite two years later, on March 2, 1938, one of the worst storms of its history visited the San Gabriel Mountains. Trestles and roadbed of the Mt. Lowe Railway were washed away.

The Pacific Electric Railway, which operated the line, requested and received permission from the State Railroad Commission to abandon the project.

The tracks were torn up, the trolleys were hauled down, the incline was scrapped and wrecked, with parts being pushed over the edge of Echo Mountain into chasms below. Collectors gathered up some historic items, others rusted or were lost with the passage of time.

Today it is difficult to conceive of the Mt. Lowe operation. With difficulty it is possible to climb the Sam Merrill Trail up Echo Mountain and see the pile of rubble that once was the cable house atop the incline. Nothing is left in Rubio Canyon. Climbing the old incline is folly: there are too many dangerous spots. It is possible to hike back along the roadbed of the old open-air trolley to the tavern site. The old shell of the tavern was dynamited and bulldozed under a few years ago.

The only remnant of the old railway today is the old cablewheel, called a bullwheel, that hauled the cars up the Echo Mountain incline. It and a suitable historical marker have been set in cement on Echo Mountain.

Thus the miracle of mountain transportation passed. It stood there grandly from 1893 to 1938. Only the knowing can stand in the Valley and point out the scars today.

XXIV <small>TRAILS</small>

There are dozens of interesting hiking trails in the San Gabriel Mountains, leading back to all manner of scenic surprises.

Trails. The origin of the many trails in the San Gabriel Mountains is various. Some were once old Indian trails, some were built by the early settlers, some were forged by mountain men, hunters, even bandits and horse thieves. During the great hiking era the building and care of trails was more deliberate and from this period most of the modern trails have evolved.

During the CCC days a large number of new trails and roads were built in the Angeles National Forest, but since then, mainly because of financial problems, few projects have been added. There is a sprinkling of these truly new trails and they are most welcomed by hikers and hiking organizations.

Some of the older trails, those dropped from the Forest Service trail system, not maintained in any form, have now become dangerous. Those of this nature listed in this chapter will be labeled dangerous. Inexperienced hikers should not attempt these unmaintained trails.

Starting, as with the roads, north of Pasadena, the first trail of note that we find is the Arroyo Seco. (See Chapter IV.)

Arroyo Seco. Access to the trail is gained at the intersection of Windsor Avenue and Ventura Street in Altadena. There is a locked gate here, but it is possible to park in the area and hike back down the road into the mouth of the Arroyo Seco. It is roughly a mile back along this gently graded road to a cluster of Forest Service residences. Here, on the outer, westernmost road, there is drinking water, a horse trough (for this is a most popular trail with horsemen) and a hitching rail. Most equestrians gain the trail from the Oak Grove Park area.

At a point one and a quarter miles from the beginning the side road up to Gould Mesa intersects. At this point along the trail there are toilets and hitching rails. This site is called the Warehouse Picnic Area.

At one time this time-battered canyon bottom road was a state highway from Pasadena to Oakwilde. Now only hikers, bicyclists, horseback riders know its charm.

Alder, willow, sycamore, bay grow along the stream bottom; canyon live oak along the canyon sides. It is a green, aromatic, pleasant spot.

A mile upcanyon from Warehouse is Nino Picnic Area. The crumbling foundations of old canyon residences are passed. The trail fords the stream several times, climbs up the east side of the canyon to get above the Brown Canyon Debris Dam, built in 1949, and about two miles above Warehouse. Then the trail drops back down behind the silted dam, onto the debris cone, reaches the old end of the road and foundations of vanished Oakwilde, a mile from the dam.

The trail then climbs up the side of the Arroyo Seco and gains— in three and a half miles—a trail camp located at the site of the vanished Switzer's resort. It is now called Commodore Switzer's Trail Camp. Here are camping facilities. There is stream water.

Following a road that is really a trail, Switzer's Campground, a mile further upstream, is gained, and from this point there is a paved road up to the Angeles Crest Highway. (See Chapter III.)

It is possible to continue hiking—or riding—on upcanyon past Upper Switzer's Campground (toilets, stoves, tables) four and a half miles to Red Box.

Side trails out of the Arroyo Seco lead up to Gould Mesa via the Edison Company road, up to the Meadows via a truck trail. The El Prieto trail takes off from the Forest Service residence area in the lower Arroyo and circles north of the Meadows, to pick up Lower Millard Canyon—roughly two miles long.

Millard Canyon. One of my favorite hikes is up Millard Canyon, which can be reached from the reservoir parking area just east of the Sunset Ridge forest station—at the end of the street named Chaney Trail in Altadena.

Actually there are two trails up Millard Canyon. The shorter, easier one, is from the bottom of lower Millard Canyon and the campground, up to the bottom of the falls—less than a mile from where it ends. The upper trail, reached from the reservoir parking area, goes on through to interesting back country.

This higher trail passes above the falls, finally gains the canyon bottom, passes the stone barrier where the trickle from the Saucer Canyon stream spills down into Millard, invades all manner of woodsy haunts, finally comes to the historic Dawn Mine, about two miles from the start.

The old mine is dangerous to explore. There are water-filled holes in the main mine tunnel, which are impossible to detect. The mine has an interesting history of gold producing, and a World War I spy ring was said to have headquartered here.

A half mile beyond Dawn Mine is the fork with Grand Canyon. On another three-quarter mile is Tom Sloan Saddle. Here is a fork in the trail, the right hand spur leading up the ridge to Mt. Lowe, three miles away. The left hand trail drops down into Bear Canyon, once a site of summer homes, but burned out in the 1959 Woodwardia Fire. From here, a mile from Tom Sloan Saddle, it is possible to follow an indistinct trail down to the Arroyo Seco where a hard-to-spot junction with the Arroyo Seco Trail is made below

103

Switzer's. If you miss the junction here you'll continue upcanyon to end at the bottom of seventy-foot Switzer's Falls, which you should not attempt to climb. There have been repeated bad accidents involving people who have tried. Three miles from Bear Canyon to the Arroyo Seco, another mile on to Switzer's.

Sam Merrill Trail. It is difficult today to describe the best method of gaining the beginning of this popular trail up to Echo Mountain from Altadena. A housing development has been chewed from the hill where the trail once ended gracefully. Now those who park in the Mount Curve Avenue-Maiden Lane area must struggle up along the Flood Control boundary fence to the beginning of the Sam Merrill Trail. Once on it, it is a gradual two and a half mile switchbacking climb to the top of Echo Mountain, way station for the old Mt. Lowe Railway. (See Chapter XXIII.)

The Sam Merrill Trail is maintained largely by a group of volunteer San Gabriel Valley folks who spend weekends keeping the historic trail in shape.

From Echo Mountain, of course, it is merely a problem of following the old Mt. Lowe Railway roadbed around its many curves, across yawning holes where trestles once stood, to the site of the vanished Alpine Tavern—four miles distant.

From the Mt. Lowe campground it is possible, too, to follow the truck trail on up the hill four more miles to the Mt. Wilson road at the Eaton Canyon Saddle. (See Chapter III.)

From this course, about a quarter mile east of the Mt. Lowe campground, a trail runs east for two miles to Idlehour trail campground in Eaton Canyon, with toilet, tables, stoves, stream water. The main trail runs on generally southeast to the Mt. Wilson Toll Road above Henniger Flats. (See Chapter V.)

It is roughly one and a half miles from Idlehour to Henniger via the Idlehour trail.

There is a firebreak-trail route from the Mt. Lowe campground to the top of Mt. Lowe. There are some slight ruins of the old tourist days still in evidence here. It was once fashionable to ride a burro from Mt. Lowe's Alpine Tavern to the summit of Mt. Lowe. That old burro trail has vanished.

For those who would follow the truck trail on up the hill to the Mt. Wilson road at Eaton Canyon Saddle, there is a trail dropping down the north side into the West Fork country to Valley Forge campground, some three miles—a good and interesting trail through some attractive timber country. Just off this trail the wreckage of a crashed airplane can be seen.

Mt. Wilson Toll Road. (See Chapter V.) From Pinecrest Drive in Altadena it is possible to walk the dirt road across the mouth of Eaton Canyon and then up the hill to Henniger Flats. It is ten miles from the bottom to Mt. Wilson—just west of the toll gate. About two miles from the top the old Mt. Wilson Trail joins in from the east.

It is a good wide trail all the way, but hardly wide enough to support the mental picture of buses and stages that used to make the climb daily.

Mt. Wilson Trail. For several years this historic old trail, the one first built by Don Benito Wilson from Sierra Madre to the summit of Mt. Wilson, was in poor condition and abandoned. In recent years a group of public spirited Sierra Madreans volunteered to rebuild the course and bit by bit it is regaining its old position as a major San Gabriel Mountains trail. Many of these volunteer trail builders are also members of the Sierra Madre mountain search and rescue group.

Park at the area near the marker commemorating the historic trail at the intersection of Mt. Wilson Trail and Miramonte Avenue in Sierra Madre and hike up the road to the trail's beginning. There are some spectacular overlooks of the Sierra Madre country from this approach up Little Santa Anita Canyon.

About four and a half miles from the bottom is Orchard Camp, once called Halfway House, where James McNally, James Beard, Foster Huston and others fashioned a resort—in its day most popular with hikers. The orchards were planted here by George Islip and George Aiken in the very early days. Captain Fred Staples was one of the early homesteaders, as was A. G. Strain.

The trail beyond Orchard Camp is still in the process of being improved by the volunteer workers. One day the old Mt. Wilson Trail will reclaim some of its lost glamor.

It is two miles from Orchard Camp to the junction with the Mt. Wilson Toll Road, switchbacked and steep along this last section.

Big Santa Anita Canyon. One of the most popular of all the trails in the mountain country, this route is sometimes known as the Sturtevant's Trail, for William M. Sturtevant, early-day mountain man, dates back to 1883, at least, when the Burlingame Brothers built the track. Later, according to historian Bill Wark, it was the first segment of the Sierra Madre-Antelope Valley Toll Trail— twenty-five cents per person to hike to the desert.

Today the trail up the Big Santa Anita is hiked by thousands each season; it is the start of the Los Angeles area Boy Scouts' Silver Moccasin Trail, which reaches all the way to Big Pines. (See Chapter VI.)

Coldbrook and Upper Bear Creek Trail. This trail starts at a point a quarter mile south of Coldbrook on State Highway 39—the Azusa to Crystal Lake road. By a series of switchbacks it climbs to the Smith Mountain Saddle and then steeply descends into Upper Bear Creek. The trail ends at a small fisherman's campground—stoves only. It is four miles up from Coldbrook to the summit, three miles down the far side.

The trail travels mainly through chaparral country, enters a region of big cone Douglas fir on its descent into the Bear Creek area. The trail is fine for equestrians.

There is normally good fishing in Upper Bear Creek where fishermen can take native rainbows. The trail is in the summer fire closure.

Windy Gap Trail. From Crystal Lake campground this pleasant trail climbs to the north to a junction with the Little Jimmy-Mt. Baden-Powell Trail. (See Chapter III.)

The trail moves up via switchback through forested country— Jeffrey pine, sugar pine, golden cup oak—passes the meadow of Big Cienega where there is drinking water. It is roughly four miles from Crystal Lake Campground to the trail junction.

This hike offers some fine overlooks of the Crystal Lake region.

Into Bear Creek. There is a "way trail"—improved only in difficult spots—up from the West Fork of the San Gabriel River into Bear Creek where by season the fishing can be good.

To reach this path park near the bridge and gate where the West Fork crosses Highway 39 just north of Rincon, and hike along the road into Cogswell Dam about a half mile to the junction of the West Fork and Bear Creek. There is a sign here indicating the upstream way trail, and this can be followed, crossing the stream variously, all the way to a fisherman's camp three miles distant. You are in the Devil's Canyon-Bear Canyon Wild Area here. By spring it is a delightful hike.

East Fork of the San Gabriel River. Baldy District Ranger Anselmo Lewis calls this a "way trail" as well, this route up from the East Fork Ranger Station along the watercourse of the East Fork of the San Gabriel River.

107

It is an interesting hike for more than fishermen—and for fishermen it gets better the further you hike.

Along the lower route there are scars of the old placer mining days to be seen. Part way up the hiker will see Swan Rock, a towering rock formation that resembles a giant swan. There are bits and pieces of the old East Fork road to be seen, a paved highway that was washed out in the 1938 flood.

It is five miles upstream to the Narrows. Here stands a long-abandoned bridge. (See Chapter VII.) There are two routes past the Narrows. One climbs via switchbacks to the old P. L. and P. Trail, that travels on and descends into Iron Fork. The other route follows the stream bottom to Iron Fork. Another route, the old Miner's Trail or Wetwater Trail, can be seen chiseled in the seep-dampened rock high above the canyon floor. It should be avoided.

Fishing is good in the Iron Fork, and beyond, in the Fish Fork. As mentioned elsewhere, this is a better hike coming downstream. Along the Blue Ridge, Prairie Fork dirt road it is possible to drive down to Cabin Flat. From here it is about a four-mile hike on down the rough road—suitable for pickups, jeeps and rugged motor scooters—to the Prairie Fork junction with Mine Gulch—where there is a fisherman's camp. Proceed on downstream past Fish Fork—with a camp—and Iron Fork, the Narrows, and out at the East Fork Forest Station. For fishermen or sightseeing hikers, this is a comfortable, interesting two-day hike. For those in a monumental hurry—and who have no business hiking here in the first place—it can be made in a day.

Along the trail the old mining complex of the Stanley Miller mine on Iron Mountain—once called Sheep Mountain—can be seen. The historic camp at Iron Fork was once known as Trogden's and there are at least two graves in the area.

Any hiker who marches up or down the East Fork must make up his mind to several stream crossings, many where it is necessary to wade. Roughly thirty of these crossings exist on the long walk from Prairie Fork to the end of the trail at the ranger station. The trail from the ranger station to the Fish Fork junction is within the summer fire closure.

In spring, or winter when there is a chance of heavy rain runoff, best check with the area ranger before trying this trek. High water in the East Fork can be a dangerous thing. It is a practical idea to check with a ranger regarding any unfamiliar trail and regarding fire closures.

Mt. Baldy Trail. There are two principal routes of climbing to the summit of Mt. Baldy. One trail leaves from the top of the Mt. Baldy chair lift, the Notch area, follows road, then trail out the Devil's Backbone and makes the narrow, crooked trail to the top of 10,064-foot Mt. Baldy.

Another route is up the fire road from the end of the county road overlooking San Antonio Falls, past Hocumac Spring to the Notch, thence up to Old Baldy.

By winter or early spring, when there is a chance of being icy patches on the shaded north side of the mountain, this route should only be taken upon approval of the area ranger or snow ranger. Steep dropoffs along this route have claimed an average of one hiker a year for the last eighteen years, and in spite of obvious posted signs, still attracts fatalities. There are some sheer, 3,000-foot dropoffs here.

Still from the top of Mt. Baldy the whole of Southern California unrolls. On a clear day by autumn or spring it is possible to see, for example, Catalina Island, Mt. San Gorgonio, Mt. San Jacinto, the Colorado River country, the southern Sierras. At this altitude both man and horse suffer and both should take it easy on the four-mile upper trail. There is no water along the upper trail from the Notch to the summit.

Photo by U. S. Forest Service

*A view of the excellent trail from Icehouse Canyon up to
Kelly's Camp in the San Antonio Canyon country.*

Icehouse Canyon. Rated by some one of the most attractive hikes in the San Gabriel range, this trail starts at the Icehouse Canyon resort up from Mt. Baldy Village. The trail first follows the Icehouse Canyon stream bottom, with water as far as Columbine Springs, then gains the Icehouse Canyon Saddle and a trail junction.

The trail to the northwest heads for Telegraph Peak and the Baldy Notch. The trail to the east reaches for Cucamonga Peak and the Cucamonga Wild Area of the San Bernardino National Forest.

The trail to the southeast leads one mile up to 8,000-foot Kelly's Camp and on to Ontario Peak, elevation 8,752 feet.

This trail, often scarred by winter avalanches, gives access to the wilderness camp at the old Kelly's Camp site. Kelly's Camp first came up prior to 1920, was later made into a tent cabin resort by Henry Delker around 1921. Cold weather and avalanches in the area in historic times have seen two hikers frozen to death, four killed by avalanches, twenty-five injured. It is a delightful hike, but not in deep winter.

From Kelly's Camp there is a trail out to the summit of Ontario Peak with its stunning vistas. There is lodgepole pine along this upper trail; in fact, Kelly's Camp, situated on a half acre beach on the side of Ontario Peak, sits in a grove of lodgepole pine. There is spring water at Kelly's Camp.

At the signed trail junction the one and a half mile hike out to Cucamonga Peak affords a view of that roadless, unimproved Wild Area. Even by the hottest days of summer, this region is cool and pine scented.

Prairie Fork area. From the Cabin Flat site down in the Prairie Fork country—access via the good dirt road from Blue Ridge—there are two motor scooter trails available to the public.

The first is down the rough Prairie Fork road from Cabin Flat to the junction of the Prairie Fork and Mine Gulch—a route unsuited for passenger cars.

The other is south from Lupine Campground up an old logging road to the top of Pine Mountain Divide and then out on a ridge between Fish Fork and Prairie Fork to a dead end. This track is fine for hunters (in season) and motor scooter enthusiasts.

Big Pines Nature Trail. Popular with Scouters and youth groups is the Big Pines Nature Trail that starts on the west side of Highway 2, directly opposite the Big Pines forest station, and climbs two and a half miles to Blue Ridge, ending at Blue Ridge Campground. Jeffrey pine, white fir, sugar pine, some incense cedar will be seen along the way. The only water is at Big Pines, and beyond Blue Ridge Campground, at Guffy Campground.

Vincent Gulch Trail. There is a trail that leaves the parking area at Vincent Saddle (Gap) and follows the stream bottom down to Prairie Fork, just above the Mine Gulch fisherman's camp. Visible on the east face of Mt. Baden-Powell is the 1900 operation of the Big Horn Mine.

Punchbowl Trail. From the South Fork Campground on the Big Rock Creek road, it is possible to scramble up over the Devil's Chair Divide and down into the strange rock formation of the Devil's Punchbowl. From the saddle there is a trail junction. The spur leads out to the commanding rock formation called the Devil's Chair. (See Chapter XI.)

Burkhart Trail. From the road end at the Lewis Ranch south from Pearblossom it is possible to find this seven-mile trail that leads up over the top of Pleasant View Ridge—and some fine pinyon pine —down into the bottom of Little Rock Canyon.

112

Buckhorn Loop. Another trail recommended for motor scooters takes off from the Buckhorn Station on the Angeles Crest Highway and climbs via an old logging road to the top of Mt. Waterman and then loops on around to the northeast to the highway again.

California Riding and Hiking Trail. The California Riding and Hiking Trail, a route that enters the area from the San Bernardino National Forest in the Wrightwood area, crosses the entire range, emerging and crossing into the Los Padres National Forest across the Old Ridge Route. Popular with equestrians and cross-country hikers, studded with small camps, this major trail is designed to traverse the entire state, first saw legislative committee discussion in 1944. The California Riding and Hiking Bill was signed into law the following year. The trail was designed to start at San Ysidro, in San Diego County, to travel north, through the San Gabriel Mountains, the Sierra Nevada, to the Oregon border, and then return via the Coast Range; a 3,000-mile loop. A map of the California Riding and Hiking Trail across Los Angeles County can be obtained from the Division of Beaches and Parks, State of California, Sacramento, California.

Fish Canyon. The Saugus District of the Angeles National Forest is cut by many lonesome canyons and unmapped arroyos that invite hiking exploration. Some of the Sawmill-Liebre country roads are excellent—and popular—for horseback riders. The main hiking trail in the area involves Fish Canyon and its tributaries.

Starting on the north at Atmore Meadows, which can be reached via a dirt road from the Sawmill-Liebre country (just off the Old Ridge Route or up from Pine Canyon Road just west of the Pine Canyon forest station) a trail leads south for one half mile and forks. The westward track leads four and a half miles to the old Gillette Mine, connects with a dirt road to the edge of the Kelly

Ranch, skirts that site via a trail, and then on the Kelly Ranch dirt access road climbs to Liebre lookout-Old Ridge Route intersection.

From the point of the fork a half mile south of Atmore Meadows, and taking the southward branch of the good trail leads four miles downstream to another trail junction at Fish Canyon. Here a left turn will return the hiker or horseman five and a half miles to the Sawmill Road via the Burnt Peak Trail. South along this canyon bottom trail will lead one fourth of a mile to Lion Camp, an excellent back country campsite for hiker or equestrian. There is a rough corral and water here, in season some forage.

Through alder, sycamore and willow the trail descends the canyon, finally reaching the scenic Narrows of Fish Canyon. The trail continues five miles from Lion Camp to Pianobox Prospect where a sometimes dirt road runs on a mile south and Cienaga Campground. From Pianobox a lesser-used trail heads northwest into the picturesque Redrock Canyon country. This three-mile stretch of trail is too steep for normal horseback travel.

Trough Canyon and Salt Creek. There is no marked trail down these watercourses, but for the experienced hiker and the mountain wise, a most interesting hike can be had by jumping off from a spur road leading east from the Old Ridge Route about three miles north of Old Reservoir Summit. From the end of this spur road, at an old oil prospect, the hiker can descend through the brush to Trough Canyon, a difficult scramble, and follow that streambed on down to the junction with Salt Creek and out then to the truck trail that runs up Cienaga Canyon. The Liebre Mountain quadrangle USGS topo map would be helpful here. It is a six-mile hike in all, and to be seen along the way are some interesting salt crystal extrusions from rock formations, some attractive pools and stream scenery. It is a recommended hike for fit nature lovers.

114

Big Oak Trail. The largest valley live oak in the world lies just off the Sierra Pelona Truck Trail out of Bouquet Canyon. (See Chapter XVI.)

Trail Canyon. This principal trail of the Tujunga region has its beginning off the Big Tujunga on the Gold Creek Truck Trail. This dirt road runs north for about a mile, past cabins, ends at a parking area. The Trail Canyon trail takes off from this point, follows the bottom of Trail Canyon for one mile to the Trail Canyon Falls. From this point the track climbs the west wall of the canyon via switchbacks, finally comes out above the sixty-foot falls.

Roughly one half mile past the falls is the Tom Lucas trail camp—stoves, tables, toilets. The trail continues up the canyon bottom two miles to Big Cienega smoking area—no camping—and here climbs up out of the defile. Two miles from Big Cienega is the Mendenhall Truck Trail which runs all the way across the Pacoima country between the Little Tujunga road to Mt. Gleason, passing Mendenhall Peak Forest Service lookout.

The Trail Canyon trail from the Big Tujunga road all the way up past Tom Lucas and Big Cienega to the Mendenhall Truck Trail and thence along that course on to Deer Springs just short of Mt. Gleason is in a special zone where hiking is allowed under permit during the season fire closure. (This, however, is subject to change depending on fire hazards.)

Trail Canyon, cutting through the semi-arid front country of the San Gabriels, is pleasantly green and watered. Wildlife leaves its tracks here, tiger lilies put on a show in the canyon bottom. Indian Ben, after whom the saddle at the trail-truck junction was named, was a prospector in the region during depression days. Tom Lucas was an early-day miner. The trail is safe for horseback riders.

Photo by U.S. Forest Service

*Off the Sierra Pelona truck trail, on a short trail, is the
largest valley live oak in the world.*

BIBLIOGRAPHY

The following sources were referred to in preparing this volume:

Trails Magazine, twenty issues, quarterly, 1934 to 1939, edited by Will H. Thrall; two issues, 1941, E. C. Bower, acting editor.

The Forest and the People, the story of the Angeles National Forest, by W. W. Robinson, Title Insurance and Trust Company, 1946.

A History of the San Gabriel Mountains, by Charles Clark Vernon, four parts, The Historical Society of Southern California Quarterly, March, June, September, December, 1956.

History of the Angeles National Forest, by S. B. Show, Regional Forester, 1945, manuscript, Angeles National Forest library.

California's Gabrielino Indians, by Bernice Eastman Johnston, Southwest Museum, 1962.

History of Pasadena, by Hiram A. Reid, Pasadena History Co., 1895.

The Southern Sierras of California, by Charles Francis Saunders, Houghton Mifflin Co., 1923.

Acton, 39, 58, 59, 62, 67
Adams, Bill; pack station, 27, 28
Agua Dulce Canyon, 63, 67
Alder Creek, 16
Aliso Canyon, 58, 62
Alpine Tavern, 10
Altadena, 12
Ancient Limber Pine Forest, 21
Angeles Crest
  Highway, 7-23, 36, 61
Angeles Forest
  Highway, 8, 57-61
Angeles Forest Mountain
  Club, 61
Angeles National Forest, 4
Antelope Valley,
  1, 7, 8, 21, 55, 57, 90
Antelope Valley Freeway, 62
Apple Tree Campground, 52
Applewhite Campground, 44
Arcadia, 27
Arroyo Seco, 7, 8, 24
Atmore Meadows, 86
Azusa, 20

Bald Mountain; weather
  station, 88, 91
Bandido Group Camp, 17
Barley Flats, 15
Beale's Cut, 69
Beale, Gen. E. F., 69
Bear Canyon, 20
Bear Canyon Road; Divide, 93
Bibliography, 117
Bichota Canyon, 35
Big Dalton Canyon, 38
Big Horn Mine, 21
Bighorn sheep, 20
Big Oaks Lodge, 73
Big Oak; Trail, 72
Big Pines;
  campground, 23, 50, 51
Big Rock Creek, 22, 52
Big Rock Campground, 22, 52
Big Santa Anita Canyon, 27, 29
Big Tujunga, 8, 59, 61, 94-97
Big Tujunga Dam, 96
Blue Ridge, 7, 22, 23
Bob's Gap Road, 52
Bouquet Canyon;
  Road, 71-74, 90
Brown Canyon Debris Dam, 8
Buckhorn Campground, 18
Buckhorn Restaurant, 40

Cajon; country;
  Pass, 1, 23, 44, 47-54
California Institute of
  Technology; Caltech, 12, 32
Call of the Canyon, 44
Camp Glenwood, 18
Camp Hi Hill, 13
Camp Pajarito, 18
Camp 37, 20
Carnegie Institution of
  Washington, 12
Cascades, 29
Castaic, 83, 84, 86
Cattle Canyon, 33, 38
Cattle Canyon ranger station, 23

Chantry, C. E., 27
Chantry Flats, 27
Charlton-Chilao Recreation
  Area, 15
Charlton Flat, 15, 16, 29
Charlton, R. H., 15
Chilao, Chilao Camp-
  ground, 16, 27, 29, 55
Christian Camp, 17
Cienega Campground, 82
Circle Mountain Ridge, 47
Cima Mesa, 54
Claremont, 42
Clear Creek, 8, 57
Cloudburst Summit, 18
Cogswell Dam, 107
Colby, Delos and Lillian, 59
Colby Ranch, 59
Coldbrook, 35
Colombo Lilac Ranch, 63
Cooper Canyon Campground, 18
Cottonwood Campground, 81
Crystal Lake, 20, 36
Crystal Lake Spur, 20
Cucamonga Peak, 42
Cucamonga Wild Area, 42
Cumorah Crest, 17

Dalton forest station, 38
Davenport Road, 63, 67
Dawson Saddle, 20
Del Sur, 90
Devil's Backbone, 41
Devil's Canyon-Bear Canyon
  Wild Area, 15, 30, 36
Devil's Punch-
  bowl, 3, 22, 47, 52
Dunham's Store, 44

Eaton Canyon Saddle, 10
Eaton Canyon, 25
Echo Mountain, 99, 100
Eldoradoville, 33
Elizabeth Lake, 90
Elizabeth Lake Canyon;
  Road, 71, 81-83
Elizabeth Lake Canyon
  Campground, 82
Elizabeth Lake Road, 89-91

Falls Campground, 73
Fern Lodge, 27
Fire Closures, 5
First ranger station, 13
Fish Canyon, 82, 83
Flores, Juan, 8
Fontana, 43
Fremont, John C, 69
Fremont Pass (See San
  Fernando Pass)

George, Abe, 8
George's Gap, 8
Glacier Campground, 40
Glendora, 38
Glendora Mountain
  Road, 33, 35, 38
Glendora Ridge Road, 38
Glenn Ranch, 44
Glenn, Silas, 43
Gold mining, 27, 32, 39, 42, 43,
  59, 62, 63, 67, 68, 81, 82, 94

Green Mountain Ranch, 44
Green Valley, 72, 76, 78, 80
Grassy Hollow Campground, 22
Grassy Mountain, 78, 80
Guffy Campground, 22

Hawkins, Nellie, 36
Henninger's Flats, 25, 26
Henniger, William K., 25
Hidden Springs, 61
Hidden Valley, 17
Hocumac Mine, 43
Hoegee's Camp; Campground, 29
Horse Flats, 17
Horse Trail Campground, 91

Ice House Canyon Resort, 40
Inspiration Point, 22
Iron Fork, 32
Iron Mountain, 15, 22
Islip Saddle, 7, 20

Jackson Flat, 22
Jackson Lake; Beach, 52
Jarvi, Sim, 21
Josephine Mountain, 8
Joshua Flat Trailer
  Campground, 55
Juniper Grove Campground, 55
Juniper Hills, 54

Kentucky Springs, 57
Knob Picnic Area, 23

La Canada, 7, 49, 57
Lake Campground, 52
Lake Hughes; Mountain
  Resort, 90
Lake Hughes Road, 81-83
Lake Tweedy, 91
Lang, 62
Largo Vista Road, 52
Leona Valley Road, 71, 89-91
Lily Springs, 37
Little Cedars Campground, 55
Little Jimmy Campground, 20
Little Jimmy Springs, 20, 37
Little Rock Campground, 17
Little Rock Creek, 17, 55
Little Rock Reservoir;
  Road, 17, 55
Little Tujunga; Road, 66, 92-93
Lodge Pole Point Area, 21
Lookouts: Josephine, 8; Vetter,
  16; West Liebre, 86
Loomis, Lester G. and Grace, 16
Loomis Ranch, 16, 17
Lone Pine Canyon, 46, 47
Los Angeles City Schools
  camp, 8
Lost Padres Mine, 59
Lowe, Thaddeus S. C., 99
Lower San Antonio Forest
  Station, 40
Lower Shake Campground, 91
Lupin Campground, 23
Lytle Creek, 39
Lytle Creek; road, 39, 43-46

Macpherson, D. J., 57, 98
Magic Mountain, 65, 93

Manker Flats, 40
Manker, Fletcher, 41
Mescal Campground, 52
Mescal Play Area, 52
Messenger Flats, 58
Mile High, 52
Mill Creek
  Summit, 17, 39, 55, 58
Mine Gulch, 23
Mint Canyon; road, 66, 67-69
Mojave Desert, 1, 21
Monrovia, 13
Morris Dam, 30, 31
Mountain Oak Campground, 52
Mt. Baden-Powell, 20, 21, 39
Mt. Baldy Lodge, 40
Mt. Baldy Park, 40
Mt. Baldy Road, 38, 39-42
Mt. Baldy Ski Lift, 41
Mt. Baldy Village, 38, 40
Mt. Disappointment, 10
Mt. Gleason, 92, 93
Mt. Hawkins, 15, 36
Mt. Islip, 15, 20, 36
Mt. Lowe, 98-100
Mt. Lowe Railway, 10, 98-100
Mt. Markham, 10
Mt. Pacifico, 17
Mt. San Antonio, 22, 38, 41
Mt. South Hawkins, 36, 37
Mt. Waterman, 15, 17, 18
Mt. Williamson, 15, 20
Mt. Wilson: peak, 10, 25; road,
  10; toll road, 10, 12, 25;
  observatory, 12, 25; trails to,
  105, 106; hotel, 12, 25
Munz Lake, 90

Newcomb's, 16
Newcomb, Louie, 16
Newcomb's Pass, 29
Nike sites, 15, 58, 65, 92, 93
Notch, The; Baldy
  Notch, 41, 46

Oak of the Golden Dream, 68
Oakwilde, 24
Oaks Picnic Area, 35
Old Baldy, See Mount San
  Antonio
Old Reservoir Summit, 86
Old Ridge
  Route, 71, 83, 84-88, 91
Ontario, 40
Opid: John, 13; Ludwik, 13
Opid's Camp, 13

Pacifico Mountain, 58
Pacoima Creek; country, 58, 92
Palmdale, 57
Palmdale Cutoff (See Angeles
  Forest Highway)
Paloma Flat, 96
Paradise Ranch, 92
Paradise Spring, 22
Peavine Campground, 52
Peck, Sedley, 33
Pianobox Prospect, 82
Pictographs, 35
Pine Canyon Dam (See
  Morris Dam)
Pine Canyon Road, 86, 89-91

Pine Hollow Picnic Area, 20
Pinyon Flats, 16, 17
Pinyon Ridge, 47
Placerita Canyon; State Park, 68
Powerhouse
  No. 1, 2, 76, 77, 78, 83
Prairie Fork, 7, 22, 23

Quail Lake Fire Station, 88

Red Box, 8, 10, 12, 13, 15
Ridge Crest Picnic Area, 20
Ridge Route, 75, 91
Rincon, 35
Roberts Camp, 27
Rock Candy Mountains, 47
Rocky Point Campground, 55
Rosenita, 17
Round Top, 58

Sahagan's, 55
St. Francis dam; disaster, 75, 76
Sandberg's, 86
San Andreas
  Fault, 3, 22, 47, 71, 88
San Antonio Canyon, 39
San Antonio Canyon Road (See
  Mt. Baldy Road)
San Bernardino National
  Forest, 4, 6, 44
Sand Canyon, 66
San Dimas Experiment
  Station, 38
San Fernando Pass, 69
San Francisquito Canyon;
  Road, 71, 72, 75-80, 83
San Gabriel Canyon
  Road, 30-37
San Gabriel Dam No. 1, 32
San Gabriel National Forest, 4
San Gabriel River, East
  Fork, 7, 21, 30, 32
San Gabriel River, North
  Fork, 30
San Gabriel River, West
  Fork, 7, 8, 12, 13, 15, 30
San Gabriel Timberland
  Reserve, 4, 13
Santa Clara River, 63, 65
Santiago Canyon, 57, 58
Sawmill Campground, 86
Sawmill-Liebre Country;
  peaks, 86, 91
Scotland Store, 44
Shady Slope Campground, 23
Shortcut Picnic Area, 15, 61
Shortcut Saddle, 15
Sierra Pelona Ridge, 67, 71
Sierra Madre, 12, 25
Sierra Madre Mountains, 1
Signal Point, 12
Singing Pines, 17
Singing Spring, 61
Ski resorts: Mt. Waterman, 18;
  Kratka Ridge, 18; Blue Ridge,
  23; Mt. Baldy, 41; Holiday Hill,
  50; Table Mountain, 50
Slover Canyon, 49
Smith Mountain, 36
Snow Crest Resort, 40
Soledad Canyon Road, 62, 93
Soledad Toll Road Company, 7

Solemint Junction, 62, 67, 68
South Fork Campground, 22, 52
South Portal Canyon, 78
Spring Camp, 13
Spunky Canyon Road, 72
Squirrel Inn, 36
Strain, A. G., 25
Strain's Camp, 12
Strawberry Peak, 8, 59
Stockton Flat, 46
Sturtevant's, 27
Sturtevant Falls, 27
Sulphur Springs
  Campground, 17
Sunland, 61
Swartout Valley, 47, 49
Switzer Campground, 8
Switzer's Camp, 8, 24
Sycamore Campground, 55
Sycamore Flats, 22, 52

Table Mountain, 47, 50
Texas Canyon, 73, 74
Thrall, Will, 43
Throop Peak, 15, 20
Thunder Mountain, 41
Tick Canyon, 68
Timberline Meadow Resort, 91
Trail Canyon, 96
Trees, record; Old Glory, 42;
  Cedar, 42; Oak, 72
Tujunga, 61
Tumble Inn, 86
Twin Oaks, 71
Twin Peaks, 15, 36
Twin Peaks Saddle, 17
Two Shay Ranch, 71

Upland, 40
U.S. Army, 40
U.S. Navy, 30, 31, 32

Valcrest, 18
Valley Forge Campgrounds, 13
Valyermo, 23, 47, 54
Vasquez Rocks, 3, 63, 68
Vasquez, Tiburcio, 8, 65
Vetter Mountain, 16
Victorville, 52
Vincent, 8, 57
Vincent Gulch, 23
Vincent Saddle;
  Gap, 7, 20, 21, 22, 35, 52
Vista Picnic Area, 18
Vogel Flat, 96

Waldron, Michael H.; tree, 21
Warm Springs Rehabilitation
  Camp, 82
West Oakdale Canyon Road, 91
White Thorn Picnic Area, 21
Wickiup Trail Camp, 61
Williams Camp, 35
Williamson, Lt. Robert
  Stockton, 20, 75
Wilson, Benjamin Davis
  (Don Benito), 25
Windy Gap, 20, 37
Winter Creek, 29
Woodwardia Canyon, 8
Wright, Sumner, 49
Wrightwood, 23, 47, 49